STOP
Studying So Much

Paul Mellor

All rights reserved. No part of this book shall be reproduced or transmitted in any form or by any means, electronic, mechanical, magnetic, photographic including photocopying, recording or by any information storage and retrieval system, without prior written permission of the publisher. No patent liability is assumed with respect to the use of the information contained herein. Although every precaution has been taken in the preparation of this book, the publisher and author assume no responsibility for errors or omissions. Neither is any liability assumed for damages resulting from the use of the information contained herein.

Copyright © 2018 by Paul Mellor

ISBN – 13: 978-0692123805

To Ben and Max

Not so fast …. you still have chores to do

To Dad, who made my study desk.

To Mom, who made all those peanut butter and jelly sandwiches that I carried to school.

Thank you for your continued love and support.

You both made learning so much fun.

Table of Contents

Introduction 1

Geography.. 6
    U.S. Capitals.. 7
    Canada... 13
    Central America.....................................15
    South America....................................... 17
    European Countries and Capitals 20
    Scandinavian Flags.................................26
    Africa 29

13 Original Colonies 38

Fun Facts 42

Presidents of the United States 43

Definitions 65

Art 72

History from A – Z 79

Remembering the Gettysburg Address 84

10 Guidelines for Giving a Speech 88

Spelling 90

Summary 124

Advanced Section 125
    Periodic Table 125

Introduction

S tudying is important. You must study to get better grades. You must study to get better in anything. Studying is vital. However, many students don't know how to study.

This book helps in becoming a better student with half the study time, because you'll be trained to look at information differently. No longer will you read information over and over hoping it 'sinks into your brain.' Instead, you'll look at information in less time and retain it. You'll create a system that will quickly get your grades on the rise.

First things first. Let's see what you already know by taking this quiz.

QUESTION: What is the capital of Oklahoma?

Austin, Topeka, Annapolis, Lansing, Oklahoma City

To find answer, unscramble the following letters.

k   o   m   a   l   h   o   a   i   c   y   t

— — — — — — — —   — — — —

Okay, tell us how you did it. Perhaps you live in Oklahoma and you already knew. Perhaps you live outside of Oklahoma and you still knew. Or, perhaps the answer was staring at you when you read the possible answers to the question. Wouldn't it be nice if every answer to every question were this easy? Perhaps they can be. This book shows how.

The key to remembering is finding a clue connecting the question to the answer. Every question provides a clue, but it's up to you to find that clue. This does not take the place of studying, but it's the way you study that makes the difference. In every test question or problem, you must ask yourself, *What do I already know?* To every question we're asked, we all know something. We may not know the answer, but we do know the question. In that question we know what was asked and we know the spelling of the words. So yes, we do know something in any question we're asked.

In the example above, you knew the question was *What is the capital of Oklahoma?* In reading that question you knew the spelling of Oklahoma. By knowing the spelling of Oklahoma, it helped you to connect that Oklahoma City is the state's capital.

2

Okay, but what about Ohio? The capital isn't Ohio City. It's Columbus, so how do we remember?

In looking at the question, *What is the capital of Ohio*, we must ask ourselves, *what do we already know*? What we know is that we have to come up with the capital of Ohio. We also know how to spell Ohio. Do you know what else we know? We know the word *Hi* is in the middle of Ohio. We also know *Hi* is surrounded by two O's. Those O*'s* look a lot like two wheels.

Do you know what else we know? We know busses have wheels, which reminds us ColumBUS is the capital of Ohio. Imagine saying Hi to a bus full of coal and you'll always remember that the capital of *oHIo* is COAL-um-BUS (Columbus).

In every question, ask yourself, *what do I already know*?

QUESTION: What are the three branches of government?

Okay, what do we already know even if we don't know the answer? We know there are three of them and we know branches are connected to trees. So, at least we know something.

The three branches of government are: Judicial, Executive, and Legislative.

How do we remember... by connecting something we know in the question to the answer.

Let's imagine branches in the tree. Branches; that's a word in the question. In the answer, we must find familiarity in the three words of Judicial, Executive, and Legislature. Let's try.

Judicial. Say it slowly and you'll almost utter *Chewed dish-el*. I can imagine a chewed dish, can you? Executive. Say this word slowly and you may say *Axe-cutive*. Hmm, there's an *axe* in there. Legislative. Oh look, I see the word *leg*. See it?

What do we already know? We know there are three branches and we know a chewed dish reminds us of Judicial; an axe reminds us of Executive, and we know the word *leg* is in Legislature.

3

Imagine an axe with a blade made from a chewed dish and a handle shaped leg cutting down branches. Close your eyes and see that image. That one visual gives you the answer to the question. When you're asked about the three branches, you'll see that axe with the chewed dish and leg handle, and you'll be reminded the three branches of government are; Judicial, Executive, and Legislative.

It's worth repeating, in every question, every chart, every painting, and every map, ask yourself, *what do I already know?*

5280 feet are in a mile

How can we remember? Hmm, what do I already know? I know I have 5 toes to each foot, and that I have 2 feet. I also know if I walk a mile, I hope I ate (8) food to put in my mouth shaped like an '0.'

Translation: 5 toes, 2 feet, 8 (ate) food that went into my mouth which is shaped as an 0. How many feet in a mile? 5,280.

Which river is longer; Amazon or Nile?

What do I already know? I know the last letter in *Amazon* is an *n*, so if I choose Amazon it's giving me a clue that my guess is incorrect. It's almost as if Amazon is whispering to me with that last letter. Psst, it begins with *n*.

Nile rhymes with mile and the Nile goes on for mile upon mile.

The 3 largest oceans

1) Pacific Ocean, 2) Atlantic Ocean, (3) Indian Ocean.

Can you spot the clues the Pacific Ocean is giving? The second letter in Pacific is A for Atlantic. Then, after the letter C is the letter I, as in Indian. In case you miss it, the Pacific gives you two *I's* to look for the Indian Ocean.

An additional clue is imagining **Pa At** the **In**n by the ocean.

How many teaspoons in a tablespoon?

Here are some clues: 3 syllables in the word *tablespoon*; 3 letters (t, a, e) are in both *tea* and *table*. 3 items are needed to consume tea at the table; cup, water, and tea.

How many teaspoons in a tablespoon? 3.

How many ounces in a cup?

Always remember, after you <u>8</u> dinner, you get an extra (b)<u>ounce</u> from a <u>CUP</u> of coffee. How many ounces in a cup? 8.

How many quarts in a gallon?

At <u>quart</u>er of, you take your <u>GALL ON **4**</u> a date. How many quarts in a gallon? 4.

Pay attention in class, ask questions, complete your assignments, and when it comes to studying, ask … What Do I Already Know?

Geography

United States Capitals

It may be a bit of a challenge to recall Iowa's capital is Des Moines or Alabama's capital is Montgomery without a memorable connection. To remember, let's link them by first creating visual images for both state and capital.

Within each state's name there is a familiar word. As an example, Florida is pronounced *Floor-ida*. We can visualize a floor. Perhaps your feet are on one now. The capital is Tallahassee. That's a word that's difficult to picture. However, when we tweak it, it becomes *tall-a-house-see*. Do you know every tall house has a floor? Of course you do, which means you also know the capital of Florida.

Study the states on the following pages by first making sure you know the state's visual clue. Then, read those memorable stories and put yourself into the picture. Each (capital city) is in parenthesis with its clue <u>underlined</u>. Soon, you'll be ready for your quiz.

7

Alabama/Ale ... <u>Ale</u> poured over <u>Mountain of Gum</u> (Montgomery)

Alaska/Lassie ... <u>Lassie</u> shakes off <u>June</u> (Juneau) bugs

Arizona/Air ... <u>Air</u> is provided to you for a small <u>Fee</u> (Phoenix)

Arkansas/Ark ... <u>Ark</u> is filled with <u>Little Rocks</u> (Little Rock)

California/Cauliflower ... <u>Cauliflower</u> dropped into <u>Sacks</u> (Sacramento)

Colorado/Color ... <u>Coloring</u> in your <u>Den</u> (Denver)

Connecticut/Cone ... <u>Cone</u> filled with <u>Hearts</u> (Hartford)

Delaware/Dollar ... <u>Dollars</u> <u>Dove</u> (Dover) into pool

Florida/Floor ... <u>Floor</u> upon floor in <u>Tall House</u> (Tallahassee)

Georgia/Jar ... <u>Jar</u> contains <u>Hat; Landed</u> (Atlanta) from above

Hawaii/Ha, Ha ... <u>Ha, Ha</u>, I own a <u>Honda</u> (Honolulu)

Idaho/Hoe ... Garden <u>Hoes</u> are used by <u>Boys</u> (Boise)

Illinois/Ill ... <u>Ill</u> patients want to <u>Spring</u> (Springfield) up

Indiana/Indians ... <u>Indians Nap</u> (Indianapolis) in <u>Indiana</u>

Iowa/Eyes ... <u>Eyes</u> are covered by <u>Dimes</u> (Des Moines)

Kansas/Can ... <u>Can</u> you stand on <u>Top and Peek</u> (Topeka)

Kentucky/Candle ... <u>Candles</u> are in <u>Frankfurters</u> (Frankfort)

Louisiana/Luge ... <u>Luge</u> is a sled driven by <u>Bats</u> (Baton Rouge)

Maine/Mane ... <u>Mane</u> is caught in <u>A gust</u> (Augusta) of wind

Maryland/Merry ... <u>Merry go round</u> riders are <u>Napping</u> (Annapolis)

Massachusetts/Matches ... <u>Matches</u> held by the <u>Boss</u> (Boston)

8

Michigan/Mesh … Mesh covers the Lantern (Lansing)

Minnesota/Mini Soda … Mini Sodas are stuck on Poles (St. Paul)

Mississippi/Sip … Sipping on a Jackknife (Jackson)

Missouri/Mow … Mowing over a Chef's (Jefferson City) hat

Montana/Mount … Mountain covered with high Heels (Helena)

Nebraska/Knob … Knob is stuck in chain Linked (Lincoln) fence

Nevada/Navel … Navel oranges drive Cars into City (Carson City)

New Hampshire/Hamster ... Hamsters eat Concord (Concord) grapes

New Jersey/New Jersey … New jerseys cover the Train (Trenton)

New Mexico/Mixing bowl … Mixing bowl of Santa's (Santa Fe)

New York/York Patty ... York Peppermint Patty is All bony (Albany)

North Carolina/No Car … No Car when you Roll (Raleigh) it over

North Dakota/Card Deck … Card Deck that Bees Mark (Bismarck)

Ohio/Hi … Say Hi to Coal on Bus (Columbus)

Oklahoma's capital is … Oklahoma City. That's easy

Oregon/Oar … Oars needed to Sail (Salem) boat

Pennsylvania/Pencil … Pencils covered with Hair (Harrisburg)

Rhode Island/Road … Roads are Paved (Providence)

South Carolina/Scarecrow … Scarecrow ran into Column (Columbia)

South Dakota/Sundeck … Sundeck covered with Pears (Pierre)

Tennessee/Tent … Tent is full of Nachos (Nashville)

Texas/Tacks … <u>Tacks</u> shoot out of <u>Exhaust</u> (Austin) system

Utah/Tar …<u>Tar</u> full of <u>Salt</u> (Salt Lake City)

Vermont/Fur … <u>Fur Peeled</u> into <u>Mounds</u> (Montpelier)

Virginia/Ginger Bread … <u>Ginger Bread</u> Man is <u>Rich</u> (Richmond)

Washington/Washing … <u>Washing Olympic</u> (Olympia) athletes

West Virginia/Vest … <u>Vest</u> is dancing the <u>Charleston</u> (Charleston)

Wisconsin/Whiz …<u>Whiz</u> kid is <u>Mad</u> (Madison)

Wyoming/YMCA … <u>YMCA</u> is filled with <u>Shy</u> (Cheyenne) people

Test your knowledge by connecting the state with its capital

New Jersey	Concord
Missouri	Topeka
Kansas	Columbus
Mississippi	St. Paul
New Hampshire	Indianapolis
Utah	Trenton
Minnesota	Sacramento
Ohio	Salt Lake City
Indiana	Jackson
California	Jefferson City

Alaska	Dover
Colorado	Atlanta
Arizona	Denver
Connecticut	Tallahassee
Alabama	Juneau
Delaware	Charleston
Georgia	Phoenix
Florida	Hartford
West Virginia	Little Rock
Arkansas	Montgomery

New York	Montpelier
South Carolina	Helena
North Dakota	Des Moines
New Mexico	Richmond
North Carolina	Santa Fe
Vermont	Raleigh
Iowa	Columbia
Wisconsin	Madison
Virginia	Albany
Montana	Bismarck

11

South Dakota	Carson City
Rhode Island	Lincoln
Louisiana	Nashville
Nevada	Springfield
Illinois	Pierre
Nebraska	Salem
Tennessee	Baton Rouge
Massachusetts	Augusta
Maine	Boston
Oregon	Providence

Which four states border each other?

Is Nebraska above Kansas or is it the other way around?

Is Tennessee above Kentucky or is Kentucky above Tennessee?

Which state borders New York; Vermont or New Hampshire?

Is Mississippi to the left or to the right of Alabama?

How quickly can you point to Iowa, Illinois, and Indiana?

Which state borders only one state?

What's the depth of the deepest Great Lake?

(See page 42 for memorable clues to these questions)

Canada

● = capital

The BRITISH (<u>British Columbia</u>) are coming ALBERT (<u>Alberta</u>), so CATCH (<u>Saskatchewan</u>) the MAN (<u>Manitoba</u>) ON (<u>Ontario</u>) the QUILT (<u>Quebec</u>)!

He FOUND a LABRADOR (Newfoundland and Labrador) named PRINCE (Prince Edward Island) whose NOSE (Nova Scotia) is BROWN (New Brunswick).

Provinces and capitals (in parenthesis)

British Columbia … <u>Brits</u> are <u>Victorious</u> (Victoria)

NOTE: Last letter in British Columbi<u>a</u> is the first letter of next province.

Alberta … <u>Albert</u> and <u>Ed</u> (Edmonton) are brothers

Saskatchewan … <u>Sasquatch</u> is in the <u>Region</u> (Regina)

Manitoba . <u>Man</u> says <u>Win a Peg</u> (Winnipeg) at the county fair

Ontario … Onto Toronto. NOTE: Each has 7 letters with many of them the same. **Ont<u>ario</u> - <u>Toro</u>nto**.

Quebec (Quebec City)

New Brunswick … A <u>Fried</u> (Fredericton) <u>Brown wick</u>

Prince Edward Island … <u>Prince Edward</u> dances with <u>Charlotte</u> (Charlottetown)

Nova Scotia … <u>No Score</u>, but still send <u>Hal a Fax</u> (Halifax).

Newfoundland and Labrador … I <u>Found a Lab</u> named <u>St. John</u>. (St. John's)

Territories and capitals (in parenthesis)

Yukon … <u>Yukon</u> can keep the <u>White horse</u> (Whitehorse)

Northwest Territories … <u>Tear</u> into it with a <u>Yellow knife</u> (Yellowknife)

Nunavut … Do you know <u>Nuns</u> <u>Quilt</u> (Iqaluit)

Central America

● = capital

The BELL (<u>Belize</u>) fell into the GUACAMOLE (<u>Guatemala</u>). I had to ELBOW (<u>El Salvador</u>) it out of the bowl then wipe it on my HONDA (<u>Honduras</u>).

I paid a kid a NICKEL (<u>Nicaragua</u>) to get it off, but he said it will COST (<u>Costa Rica</u>) more. I disagreed and he hit me over the head with a frying PAN (<u>Panama</u>). I should have paid him more.

Central American Capitals (underlined)

Belize's capital is <u>Belmopan</u>. Note: Same beginning three letters in both country and capital. The word *mop* is in Bel*mop*an. Think of a *Bell* with a *Mop* on it.

Guatemala's capital is <u>Guatemala City</u>. To remember the spelling, imagine saying the following to your friend: **G**, **U ATE** (at the) **MAL**(L).

Honduras' capital city is <u>Tegucigalpa</u>. Imagine a <u>tug</u>boat, similar to *Teg*, pulling your *Honda*. To remember the spelling, imagine **U C i**ncredible **GAL** with her **PA**.

El Salvador's capital is <u>San Salvador</u>. Not sure which is which? Remember that *country* is pronounced *countreeee*. The *count*r*eeee* is *E*l Salvador.

Nicaragua's capital is <u>Managua</u>. Imagine a <u>Man</u> named Nick. NOTE: Same last three letters in both country and capital. Also, one more stroke in the letter *N* (for *N*icaragua) and it becomes an *M* (for *M*anagua).

Costa Rica's capital is <u>San Jose</u>. You just can't walk out of a store with a garden *hoe* (Hoe-say). It <u>cost</u> (Costa Rica) money.

Panama's capital is <u>Panama City</u>.

South America

● = capital

I was in BRAZIL (Brazil), you know, **South America**, when I met this FRENCH GIRL, ANA (French Guiana). She asked, SIR what is your NAME (Suriname)? I answered GUY, ANA (Guyana).

She said she had taken a TRAIN and a TOBOGGAN (Trinidad and Tobago), then a VAN (Venezuela), which made her very COLD (Columbia) and hungry. So HECK, I opened the DOOR (Ecuador) and she began to PURR (Peru). I offered her a BOWL (Bolivia) of PEARS (Paraguay).

She said YOU GUY (Uruguay) are very nice. You ARE a GENTLEMAN (Argentina). I'm no longer CHILLY (Chili).

The moral of the story: when you come to the FORK (Falkland Islands) in the road to being mean or nice; choose nice.

17

South American Capitals (underlined)

Brazil's capital is Brasilia. Same first 3 letters.

French Guana's capital is Cayenne. (Kie-anne)
<u>Kile</u> and <u>Ann</u> (Cayenne) share a <u>French</u> (French Guana) fry.

Suriname's capital is Paramaribo.
At the zoo you ask, Hey <u>Pa</u>, what's that <u>Ram</u>'s (Paramaribo), <u>Sur Name?</u>
(Suriname)

Guyana's capital is Georgetown.
<u>Guy's</u> (Guyana) name is <u>George</u> (Georgetown).

Trinidad and Tobago's capital is Port-of-Spain.
Visualize a <u>Train</u> or a <u>Toboggan</u> (Trinidad and Tobago) pulling up to a <u>Port</u>
(Port-of-Spain).

Venezuela's capital is Caracas. (car-rock-us)
Should we go by <u>Van</u> (Venezuela) or <u>Car</u> (Caracas)?

Columbia's capital is Bogota.
<u>Bow</u> hits <u>Guitar</u> (Bow Guitar) full of <u>Coal</u> (Columbia).

Ecuador's capital is Quito (key-toe).
When you <u>Exit Door</u> (Ecuador) you lock with <u>Key</u> with <u>Toe</u> (Quito).

Peru's capital is Lima.
<u>Lee</u> and <u>Ma</u> (Lima) like <u>Pears</u> (Peru).

Bolivia's capital is Sucre. (Soo-kra).
<u>Bowl</u> (Bolivia) of <u>Soothing Crayfish</u> (Sucre).

Paraguay's capital is Asunciòn.
<u>Para</u> (Paraguay) sailing near the <u>Sun</u> (Asunciòn).

Uruguay's capital is Montevideo.
A <u>Mound of Videos</u> (Montevideo) on your <u>Rug</u> (Uruguay).

Argentina's capital is Buenos Aires.
Gentle Tina (Argentina) is Beautiful (Buenos). She has an Air (Aires) about her. Also, the first and last letter of Argentina are both A's; for Aires.

Chili's capital is Santiago.
Santa (Santiago) gets Chilly (Chili).

Falkland Islands' capital is Stanley.
Stainless steel Forks (Falkland Islands) or Standing Forks.

European Countries & Capitals

The country and capital are slightly changed into memorable images.
The (capital city) is in parenthesis. Read each sentence slowly and visual
what is happening. It will help you to remember.

Albania/Album ... <u>Tears</u> (Tirana) fall on cover of <u>Album</u>

Austria/Horse-tria ... <u>Horse</u> ate <u>Vienna</u> (Vienna) sausages

Belgium/Bell ... <u>Bell</u> is full of <u>Brussels</u> (Brussels) sprouts

Belarus/Bell rust ... <u>Mink</u> (Minsk) coat hidden in <u>Rusted Bell</u>

Bosnia/Bars knee ... <u>Sara</u> (Sarajevo) dropped the <u>Bars on her Knee</u>

Bulgaria/Bulk ... <u>Sofas</u> (Sofia) bought in <u>Bulk</u>

Croatia/Crow ... <u>Crows</u> <u>Zig Zag</u> (Zagreb) in flight

Cyprus/ Cyprus ... <u>Cyprus</u> trees dropped <u>Nickels</u> (Nicosia)

Czech Republic/Checks ... <u>Pray</u> (Prague) the <u>Checks</u> come

Denmark/Den ... <u>Co pens</u> (Copenhagen) are in the <u>Den</u>

Estonia/Tone ... <u>Tall inn</u> (Tallinn) is full of <u>Tone</u> bodies

Finland/Fin ... Stuck my <u>Heel</u> (Helsinki) into shark's <u>Fin</u>

France/Frown ... Here, eat a <u>Pear</u> (Paris) and don't <u>Frown</u>

Germany/Germ ... If you're <u>Burr</u> (Berlin) you'll get <u>Germs</u>

Greece/Grease ... <u>Thin</u> (Athens) the <u>Grease</u>

Hungary/Hungry ... <u>Buddy, you pest</u> (Budapest). I'm <u>Hungry</u>

Iceland/Ice ... <u>Ice</u> needs to be <u>Raked</u> (Reykjavik)

Ireland/Eye ... <u>Dab</u> (Dublin) your <u>Eye</u>

Italy/It ... <u>It</u> <u>Roams</u> (Rome) in Italy

Kosovo/Cove … <u>Cove</u> was very <u>Pristine</u> (Pristina)

Latvia/Latch … <u>Latch</u> the <u>Rig</u> (Riga)

Lithuania/Lit … <u>Villain</u> (Vilnius) <u>Lit</u> the match

Luxembourg is the capital of … Luxembourg

Macedonia/Ma said … <u>Ma said</u> use <u>Scope</u> (Skopje) mouthwash

Malta/Malt … <u>Malt</u> spilled into <u>valley. Let</u> it (Valletta)

Moldova/Mold … <u>Mold</u> had to be <u>Chiseled</u> (Chisinau) away

Montenegro/Mountain … <u>IPod</u> (Podgorica) lost on the <u>Mountain</u>.

Netherlands/Net … <u>Ham, by Dam</u> (Amsterdam), is in <u>Net</u>

Norway/No Way … <u>No way</u> will I let <u>Ozzie go</u> (Oslo)

Poland/Pole … <u>Poles</u> used by <u>Warriors</u> (Warsaw)

Portugal/Port Gal … Beautiful <u>Lips</u> (Lisbon) on <u>Gals at Port</u>

Romania/Romaine ... <u>Boo! Rest</u> (Bucharest) on <u>Romaine</u> lettuce

Serbia/Slurp ... He <u>Slurped</u> in a <u>Bell</u> of <u>Grade</u> A (Belgrade) milk

Slovakia/Slow vacuum ... <u>Brat</u> (Bratislava) is using my <u>Slow Vac</u>

Slovenia/Slow van ... <u>Job</u> went to <u>Jana</u> (Ljubljana) in <u>Slow Van</u>

Spain/Spine … Crooked <u>Spine</u> makes me <u>Mad</u> (Madrid)

Sweden/Sweet … <u>Stock homes</u> (Stockholm) with <u>Sweets</u>

Switzerland/Swat … <u>Swat</u> the <u>Burning</u> (Bern) fly

Turkey/Turkey …<u>Turkey</u> breaks its <u>Ankle</u> (Ankara)

Ukraine/Crane … <u>Crane</u> lifts heavy <u>Key</u> (Kiev)

United Kingdom/King ... <u>Kings</u> of the jungle are <u>Lions</u> (London)

NOTE: Although a part of Russia, the small area between Poland and Lithuania is the City of Kaliningrad.

Connect the country with its capital

Macedonia	Paris
France	Bucharest
Kosovo	Vienna
Austria	Skopje
Romania	Madrid
Spain	Pristina

- -

Bulgaria	Bern
Moldova	Reykjavik
Iceland	Kiev
Switzerland	Chisinau
Slovenia	Sofia
Ukraine	Ljubljana

Netherlands	Sarajevo
Hungary	Amsterdam
Croatia ——————————Zagreb	
Bosnia	Rome
Malta	Budapest
Italy	Valletta

Finland	Stockholm
Sweden	Vilnius
Lithuania	Helsinki
Cyprus	Tirana
United Kingdom	Nicosia
Albania	London

Greece	Podgorica
Montenegro	Belgrade
Poland	Riga
Serbia	Ankara
Turkey	Warsaw
Latvia	Athens

Belgium	Berlin
Czech Republic	Prague
Denmark	Tallinn
Estonia	Brussels
Germany	Dublin
Ireland	Copenhagen
Portugal	Lisbon

What's the order of those Seas?

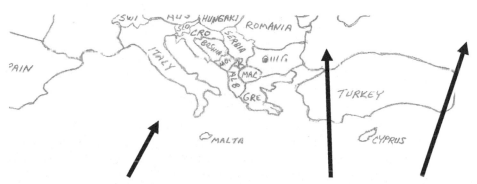

The <u>MED</u> (**Mediterranean**) student, Mr. <u>BLACK</u>, (**Black**) can <u>C</u> (**Caspian**) you now.

Scandinavian Flags

The flags of Iceland, Norway, Sweden, Finland, and Denmark look alike, especially when viewing them here in black and white. Each has a similar design, but the colors are different.

ICELAND. As a hint, think of the <u>RED CROSS</u> putting <u>ICE</u> (Iceland) on your wound. The background is <u>blue</u>. Think Blue Ice. A <u>white</u> border separates the colors.

NORWAY. The design of the Norwegian flag is similar to Iceland's. However, the reds and blues have been switched. The flag of Norway has a RED background. Note the letter *R* in No*R*way.

Also, imagine saying to your insurance friend, "I <u>NO</u> (as in *know*) you work for BLUE CROSS Insurance.

SWEDEN. The Swedish flag has a YELLOW cross on a blue field. It looks like a yellow brick road on a blue canvas. That's <u>Sweet-ish</u>.

DENMARK. The Danish flag looks like a beautiful gift in a red box with a WHITE ribbon. Let's put that in the DEN (Denmark).

FINLAND. The flag of Finland looks like a huge airplane. Note the wider stripe compared to the other flags. Those wings look like fins; blue fins soaring through the white cloud.

Your mother gave you an **icy** (Iceland) stare saying **No Way** (Norway) will you eat **sweets** (Sweden) before you **finish** (Finland) your **dinner** (Denmark).

Africa

In his remarks about his former collegue at CBS News, Andy Rooney spoke about the brillance of Harry Reasoner, who had recently passed away. Rooney said Harry had a great memory and on a blank map could fill in all African countries.

The following eight pages shows how you can be just like Harry.

To simplify our work, we divide Africa into six regions. The first region includes ten countries, beginning in the northwest part of the continent that follows the coastline of the Atlantic Ocean.

Next, each country's name will be slightly altered into a familiar word or phrase, then woven into a story helping us to remember.

29

Region I

1. Morocco
2. Western Sahara
3. Mauritania
4. Senegal
5. Gambia

6. Guinea-Bissau
7. Guinea
8. Sierra Leone
9. Liberia
10. Côted d'Ivoire

More rocks (Morocco) washed up on the *western shore* (Western Sahara); *more tan* (Mauritania) than anything else. I *sent a gal* (Senegal) to get them. She thought it was a *game* (Gambia). She felt like a *guinea pig; a busy* (Guinea-Bissau) *guinea* (Guinea) pig. Her name was *Sierre Leone* (Sierra Leone). I'm not *lying* (Liberia). She was *coated with ivory* (Côted d' Ivoire).

30

<u>Region II</u>

This region begins in the northern most country and moves to the east (right) ending at the Red Sea.

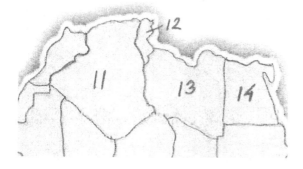

11. Algeria
12. Tunisia
13. Libya
14. Egypt

When I saw *Algae* (<u>Algeria</u>) had covered the *tuna's* (<u>Tunisia</u>) *lip* (<u>Libya</u>), I got in my *Jeep* (<u>Egypt</u>) and drove off.

Region III

Nine countries, beginning inland above Côte d'Ivoire (#10), in the western part of Africa. The pathway continues east to the coast. Once at the coast, the path drops to #21, then moves to the east and finishes at the dot (#23).

Familarize the route by tracing it with your finger.

NOTE: Mali (#15) is shaped like an upside down letter *M*; as in Mali.

15. Mali
16. Burkina Faso
17. Niger
18. Chad
19. Sudan

20. Eritrea
21. Ethopia
22. Somalia
23. Djibouti

At the *mall* (Mali) it got *burr fast* (Burkina Faso). My friend *Niger* (Niger), *Chad* (Chad), and the inseparable Sue and Dan, known as *Sudan* (Sudan), warmed me up with the *right tea* (Eritrea). It was almost like *ether* (Ethiopia) used to put people to sleep. I had *insomnia* (Somalia) until a *DJ, about* (Djibouti) time, played music to wake me.

32

Region IV

Beginning on the Atlantic coast to the immediate right of Côte d'Ivoire (#10), the path manuevers around many small countries. Study the route.

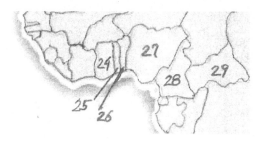

24. Ghana
25. Togo
26. Benin
27. Nigeria
28. Camcroon
29. Central African Republic

I was a *gonna* (<u>Ghana</u>), because it was time *to go* (<u>Togo</u>) see *Ben in* (<u>Benin</u>) *Nigeria* (<u>Nigeria</u>). I brought my *camera* (<u>Cameroon</u>) and drove away in my *c.a.r.* (<u>Central African Republic</u>).

CLUE: Notice <u>Nige</u>ria is directly below <u>Niger</u>.

Region V

Nine countries make up this region. Start at one small country (#30) and finish up at two others, with the reminder that *B* comes before *R* (*Bu*R*undi*).

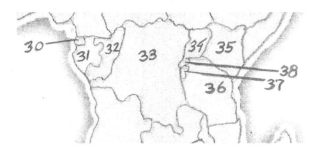

30. Equatorial Guinea
31. Gabon
32. Republic of the Congo
33. Democratic Republic of the Congo
34. Uganda
35. Kenya
36. Tanzania
37. Burundi
38. Rwanda

Don't toss any *eggs* (eg – Equatorial Giunea) or *gab on* (Gabon). Just come out and say, Hey, *Republicans* (Republic of the Congo) and *Democrats of the Congo* (Democratic Republic of the Congo), *you again* (Uganda), *can ya* (Kenya) get along? Get some *tans* (Tanzania); *B U-tiful* (*Bu-rundi*) (Burundi) ones. Don't you *wanna* (Rwanda)?

Region VI

This region covers the southern portion of Africa. Beginning at #39 (Angola) on the west coast, the route finishes at the island of Madagascar.

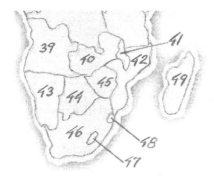

39. Angola
40. Zambia
41. Malawi
42. Mozambique
43. Namiba
44. Botswana

45. Zimbabwe
46. South Africa
47. Lesotho
48. Swaziland
49. Madagascar

Angel, (<u>Angola</u>), dress like a *Zombie* (<u>Zambia</u>) to scare my *ma, the lawyer* (<u>Malawi</u>). She's a lawyer, but *mows them big* (<u>Mozambique</u>) yards. She can't *name* (<u>Namibia</u>) any of of her customers, except the guy who *bought that wannabe* (<u>Botswana</u>) mansion. Mr. *Zimmer; Bob* (<u>Zimbabwe</u>) is his first name. He's from *South Africa* (<u>South Africa</u>). He spends *less though* (<u>Lesotho</u>) living there than when he lived in *Switzerland* (<u>Swaziland</u>). He used to be *mad* about that high cost of living. He told me that when he was *gassing* up his *car* (<u>Madagascar</u>).

Fill in the missing country

Guinea, Gambia, Senegal
Liberia, Morocco, Western Sahara, Mauritania,
Côted d' Ivoire, Guinea-Bissau, Sierra Leone,

More rocks (_____) washed up on the *western shore* (_____); *more tan* (_____) than anything else. I had to *send a gal* (_____) to get them. She thought it was a *game* (_____) I was playing with her. She felt like a *guinea pig; a busy* (_____) *guinea* (_____) pig. Her name was *Sierre Leone* (_____) . I'm not *lying* (_____). She was *coated with ivory* (_____).

Tunisia, Libya, Egypt, Algeria

When I saw *Algae* (_____) had covered the *tuna's* (_____) *lip* (_____), I got in my *Jeep* (_____) and drove away.

Somalia, Sudan, Burkina Faso, Djibouti,
Eritrea, Ethiopia, Mali, Niger, Chad

At the *mall* (_____) it got *burr fast* (_____). I was cold. My friend *Niger* (_____), *Chad* (_____), and the inseparable Sue and Dan, known as *Sudan* (_____), warmed up with the *right tea* (_____). It was almost like *ether* (_____) used to put people to sleep. I had *insomnia* (_____) until a *DJ, about* (_____) time, played music to wake me.

Benin, Central African Republic,
Ghana, Togo, Cameroon, Nigeria

I was a *gonna* (_____) because it was time *to go* (_____) see *Ben in* (_____) *Nigeria* (_____). I brought my *camera* (_____) and drove away in my *c.a.r* (_____).

Democratic Republic of the Congo, Rwanda, Kenya, Equatorial Guinea, Tanzania, Uganda, Gabon,Republic of the Congo, Burundi,,

Don't toss any *eggs* (_____) or *gab on* (_____). Just come out say it: Hey, *Republicans* (_____) and *Democrats of the Congo* (_____), *you again* (_____), *can ya* (_____) get along? Get some *tans* (_____); *B U-tiful* (_____) ones. Don't you *wanna* (_____)?

Zimbabwe, Malawi, Madagascar, Zambia, Namibia, Angola, Botswana, Mozambique, South Africa, Swaziland, Lesotho

Hi *Angel* (_____), go and dress like a *Zombie* (_____) and scare my *ma, the lawyer* (_____). Yes, she's a lawyer. But she just *mows them big* (_____) yards one right after another. She can't *name* (_____) any of of her customers, except the guy who *bought that wannabe* (_____) mansion. Mr. *Zimmer; Bob* (_____) is his first name. He's from *South Africa* (_____). He spends *less though* (_____) living there than when he lived in *Switzerland* (_____). He used to be *mad* about that high cost of living. He told me that when he was *gassing* up his *car* (_____).

13
Original Colonies

B elow are the 13 original colonies in the order they were admitted to the union.

Delaware

Pennsylvania

New Jersey

Georgia

Connecticut

Massachusetts

Maryland

South Carolina

New Hampshire

Virginia

New York

North Carolina

Rhode Island

What are you going to do to learn them? Are you going to say them over and over hoping that by the 19th reciting you'll have them 'down cold?'

That's what I used to do. Trouble was, by the time I sat in class to take the test my brain froze, and I couldn't remember. It also didn't help that I spent my childhood in one of those 13 colonies.

I'd say these states over and over without asking myself, *what do I already know*?

What I knew was that the books and television shows I enjoyed the most involved stories. I could remember stories. There wasn't one TV show that aired only a group of words.

Remember, stories are memorable; lists are not. Using the helpful hints for states on pages 8-10, you'll see how easier it is to recall the colonies.

Delaware to **Pennsylvania** to **New Jersey**

Imagine <u>DOLLARS</u> wrapped around a giant <u>PENCIL</u>. Then, imagine those pencils piercing that <u>NEW JERSEY</u> of yours. Your new jersey is full of holes from all those sharp pointed pencils.

(New Jersey) to **Georgia** to **Connecticut**

Imagine stuffing your new jersey into a <u>JAR</u>. Push the entire jersey into the jar. Make it fit. Afterward, make that jar into a huge ice cream <u>CONE</u>. That's weird. Why is that boy using a jar as an ice cream cone?

(Connecticut) to **Massachusetts** to **Maryland** to **South Carolina**

Pretend you're holding the cone and you light a MATCH. The matches ignite a fire into the cone. The fire spreads to the MERRY-GO-ROUND where all the SCARECROWS are enjoying a ride. Get them off, they'll burn.

(South Carolina) to **New Hampshire** to **Virginia**

Poor Scarecrow. He jumps about as his straw is flying off. Fortunately, a kind HAMSTER gathers the loose straw and returns it to the owner. In return the hamster is rewarded with a tasty GINGER BREAD MAN. Yum!

(Virginia) to **New York** to **North Carolina** to **Rhode Island**

Amazingly, the ginger bread man comes to life, and after eating a YORK PEPPERMINT PATTY, drives off in a CAR down the RHODE.

List the colonies in the order they joined the union. Below are your clues.

Scarecrow, Dollar, Road, Car, York Peppermint Patty,
Merry Go Round, Jar, Cone, Match, New Jersey, New Hamster,
Pencil, Ginger Bread Man

_____

_____

_____

_____

_____

_____

_____

_____

_____

_____

_____

_____

_____

Fun Facts

What's the largest country in South America? Be BRAVE. It's Brazil.

What's the capital of New Zealand? If you can imagine a SEAL swimming in the WELL it may help you to know that Wellington is the capital of New Zealand (Seal-land).

What's the capital of Australia? If you take a hike on a TRAIL (Aus-TRAIL-ia) you'll want to bring with you a CAN of BERRIES (Canberra).

What's the capital of China? Before I tell you, please, never throw your fine CHINA into the BAY (Beijing).

Utah, Colorado, Arizona, and New Mexico make up the four corner states. To remember, *U C A Mixing* Bowl in every corner. I see it.

Nebraska is above Kansas. To remember, the last two letters of Nebras-<u>KA</u> lead into the spelling of the state directly below.

Kentucky is above Tennessee. As a reminder, *K* comes before *T*, not only in the alphabet, but also in the name *KenT*ucky.

New York is not one of the New England states. Note how the *V*, as in *V*ermont, acts as a wedge separating the state from northern New England.

I MISS AL, don't you? Mississippi's on the left of Alabama.

EYES are ILL, IN the hospital I go. Iowa, Illinois, and Indiana are right in a row.

The state with one syllable also borders one state; Maine.

It's SUPERIOR to the other Great Lakes in depth. This <u>1</u> Lake, which borders <u>3</u> states, has a maximum depth of <u>1333</u>.

Presidents
of the
United States
of America

I, (____your name____), do solemnly swear that I will faithfully execute the reading of this chapter, and will to the best of my ability, preserve, protect, and remember the information in this section.

They were farmers, lawyers, and soldiers. They came from places such as Niles, North Bend, and New York City, and had names such as, Roosevelt and Reagan; Coolidge and Cleveland; and Johnson and Johnson.

They were college graduates and school dropouts, who had one thing in common – they rose to hold the highest office in the land.

These are the Presidents of the United States of America; forty-four men who have made their mark in World History.

Do you know who they are? If not, you soon will. Not even an executive order can cause you to forget.

How do you do that? It's easy. We're going to turn Presidents into pictures and turn numbers into memorable images. It's fun to do, but it takes your imagination. You have an imagination, don't you? You're not sure? Okay, let's find out. Can you visualize a huge elephant jumping atop a fire truck in the pouring rain? You can? Great. You passed the test.

This is the number 1. Take a good look at it. Are you impressed? Probably not. It's boring. It doesn't move. It just stands there and does nothing. If you stare at it long enough it may put you asleep.

Now, look at this pencil which resembles the number 1.

Can you almost feel it? Can you imagine sharpening it and then writing? Unlike the number 1, the pencil has a smell and a feel to it, and when writing it glides across the page. It's that movement that makes the pencil more memorable than the number.

On the following pages, numbers 1 – 45, representing the Presidents, are transposed to pictures. Carefully study each picture and you'll see a number within the picture. Some picturesque numbers you'll see instantly, such as the *diving board* for number 7 or *keys* for number 30.

Others may be slightly hidden, but they are very present, such as number 36 in the *cherries*; number 37 in the *bananas*; the number 4 inside the *bulb* for number 40; and the eyes of the *pumpkin*, shaped like 4's, in number 40.

Spend time learning these pictures. It's new to you now, but with practice you'll automatically associate *antelope* with #41, and *snowman* with #8. Trace the number with your fingertip. That helps.

Picturesque Numbers

1 = Pencil

6 = Golf Club

2 = Swan

7 = Diving Board

3 = Pitchfork

8 = Snowman

4 = Sailboat

9 = Flagpole

5 = Saxophone

10 = Bat and Ball

11 = Ladder

16 = Stump and Ax

12 = Ear

17 = Door

13 = Harp

18 = Doughnuts

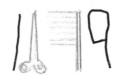

14 = Goal Post

19 = Scissors and Comb

15 = Shoes

20 = Lasso

21 = Elephant Foot

26 = Boot and Spur

22 = Fortune Cookie

27 = Teapot

23 = Fish

28 = Juggler

24 = Bird and its House

29 = Intestines/Lollypop

25 = Couple Kissing

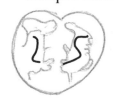

30 = Keys

31 = Squirrel

36 = Cherries

32 = Plug and Cord

37 = Bananas

33 = Frogs

38 = Handcuffs

34 = Umbrella

39 = Hairdryer

35 = Flame and Pipe

40 = Lightbulb

41 = Antelope

42 = Swimmers

43 = Nose and Lips

44 = Pumpkin

45 = Speed Limit Sign

Review

What number is represented by a *Pencil*?
Is it number **1**, **12**, or **9**?
Write answer here _____

What number is represented by a *Teapot*?
Is it number **14**, **27**, or **17**?
Write answer here _____

What number is represented by *Frogs*?
Is it number **38**, **22**, or **33**?
Write answer here _____

Draw a line to the corresponding picture

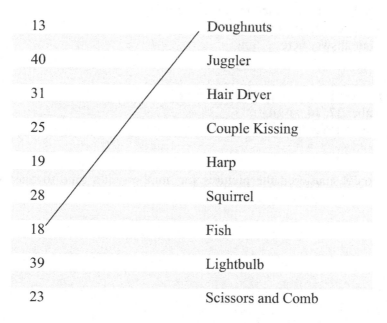

13	Doughnuts
40	Juggler
31	Hair Dryer
25	Couple Kissing
19	Harp
28	Squirrel
18	Fish
39	Lightbulb
23	Scissors and Comb

Write the number translating to the correct picture.

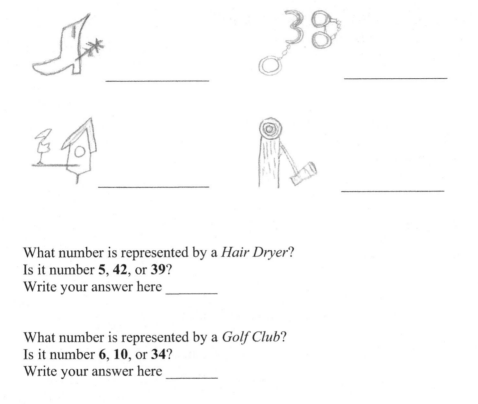

What number is represented by a *Hair Dryer*?
Is it number **5**, **42**, or **39**?
Write your answer here _____

What number is represented by a *Golf Club*?
Is it number **6**, **10**, or **34**?
Write your answer here _____

What number is represented by *Bananas*?
Is it number **37**, **26**, or **20**?
Write your answer here _____

Once you've mastered the pictures for numbers, it's time to master the pictures for Presidents.

Presidential Connection

Each President's name is altered creating a memorable visual. For instance, *Tyler* converts to a *Tie*, as in *Tie-ler* and *Carter* translates to *Cart-er*. These pictures are associated into the picture number. This crazy, bizarre image will help you remember all the Presidents.

1 George Washington

1 translates to *Pencil*
Washington translates to *Washing Machine*

Pencils sticking through the *Washing Machine*.

2 John Adams

2 translates to *Swan*
Adams translates to *Apple*

Swan becomes part *Apple*

3 Thomas Jefferson

3 translates to *Pitchfork*
Jefferson translates to *Chef's Hat*

Pitchforks attacking *Chef's Hat*

4 James Madison

4 translates to *Sailboat*
Madison translates to *Mud*

Sailboat covered in *Mud*

5 James Monroe

5 translates to *Saxophone*
Monroe translates to *Money*

Money flowing from *Saxophone*

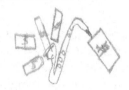

6 John Quincy Adams

6 translates to *Golf Club*
Quincy Adams translates to *(Q) Ball*

Q Ball struck by *Golf Club*

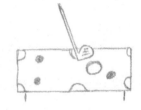

7 Andrew Jackson

7 translates to *Diving Board*
Jackson translates to *Jackhammer*

Jackhammer jumping from *Board*

8 Martin Van Buren

8 translates to *Snowman*
Van Buren translates to *Van*

Snowman riding in *Van*

9 William Henry Harrison

9 translates to *Flagpole*
Harrison translates to *Hair*

Hair flying from *Flagpole*

10 John Tyler

10 translates to *Bat and Ball*
Tyler translates to *Tie*

Tie with *Baseballs*

11 James K. Polk

11 translates to *Ladder*
Polk translates to *Polka Dot Dress*

Polka Dot Dress on *Ladder*

12 Zachary Taylor

12 translates to *Ear*
Taylor translates to *Tail*

Dog's Tail stuck in *Ear*

13 Millard Fillmore

13 translates to *Harp*
Fillmore translates to *Film*

Film stuck in a *Harp*

14 Franklin Pierce

14 translates to *Goal Post*
Pierce translates to *Pierced Earrings*

Goal Post with *Pierced Earrings*

15 James Buchanan

15 translates to *Shoes*
Buchanan translates to *Cannon*

Shoes fired from *Cannon*

16 Abraham Lincoln

16 translates to *Axe leaning against stump*
Lincoln translates to *Sausage Links*

Sausage Links cut by an *Axe*

17 Andrew Johnson

17 translates to *Door*
Johnson translates to *Toilet Paper from Porta-John*

Toilet Paper wrapped around *Door*

18 Ulysses S. Grant

18 translates to *Doughnuts*
Grant translates to *Ant*

Ant walking off with *Doughnuts*

19 Rutherford B. Hayes

19 translates to *Hair Cutting Tools*
Hayes translates to *Haystack*

Haystack of *Hair Cutting Tools*

20 James Garfield

20 translates to *Lasso*
Garfield translates to *Garlic*

Lassoing Garlic

21 Chester A. Arthur

21 translates to *Elephant's Foot*
Arthur translates to *Art Show*

Elephant advertising *Art Show*

22 Grover Cleveland

22 translates to *Fortune Cookies*
Cleveland translates to *Clover*

Clover in *Fortune Cookies*

23 Benjamin Harrison

23 translates to *Fish*
Benjamin Harrison translates to *Hair*

Bony Fish with *Hair* (<u>Bone</u>-jamin <u>Hair</u>-ison)

24 Grover Cleveland

24 translates to *Birdhouse*
Cleveland translates to *Clover*

Clover at *Birdhouse*

25 **William McKinley**

25 translates to *Couple Kissing* *McKinley* translates to *Monkey*

Kissing Monkey

26 **Theodore Roosevelt**

26 translates to *Boot and Spur* *Roosevelt* translates to *Rose*

Boot with *Rose* spur

27 **William Howard Taft**

27 translates to *Teapot* *Taft* translates to *Taffy*

Taffy stuck on *Teapot*

28 **Woodrow Wilson**

28 translates to *Juggler* *Wilson* translates to *Wheels*

Juggler on *Wheels*

29 **Warren G. Harding**

29 translates to *Intestines and Lollypop* *Harding* translates to *Heart*

Heart holding a *Lollypop*

30 Calvin Coolidge

30 translates to *Keys*
Coolidge translates to *Cooler*

Cooler full of *Keys*

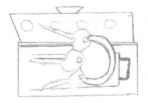

31 Herbert Hoover

31 translates to *Squirrel*
Hoover translates to *Hoover Vacuum Cleaner*

Squirrel vacuuming with *Hoover Vacuum*

32 Franklin Roosevelt

32 translates to *Plug and Cord*
Roosevelt translates to *Rose*

Plug with *Rose* cord

33 Harry Truman

33 translates to *Frogs*
Truman translates to *True*

Frogs who are *True*

34 Dwight D. Eisenhower

34 translates to *Umbrella*
Eisenhower translates to *Eyes*

Eyes covering *Umbrella*

35 John F. Kennedy

35 translates to *Flame and Pipe*
Kennedy translates to *Can*

Trash Can smoking *Pipe*

36 Lyndon Johnson

36 translates to *Cherries*
Johnson translates to *Toilet Paper from Porta-John*

Cherries wrapped around *Toilet Paper*

37 Richard Nixon

37 translates to *Bananas*
Nixon translates to *Nickel*

Bananas flipping *Nickels*

38 Gerald Ford

38 translates to *Handcuffs*
Ford translates to *Fort*

Handcuffs on *Fort*

39 Jimmy Carter

39 translates to *Hair Dryer*
Carter translates to *Cart*

Cartful of *Hair Dryers*

40 Ronald Reagan

40 translates to *Light Bulb*
Reagan translates to *Rake*

Raking Light Bulbs

41 George Bush

41 translates to *Antelope*
Bush translates to *Bush*

Antelope in *Bush*

42 Bill Clinton

42 translates to *Swimmers*
Clinton translates to *Clown*

Swimming Clown

43 George W. Bush

43 translates to *Nose and Lips*
Bush translates to *Bush*

Nose and Lips along *Bush*

44 Barack Obama

44 translates to *Pumpkin*
Obama translates to *Bomb*

Bomb blowing up *Pumpkin*

45 **Donald Trump**

45 translates to *45mph Sign*
Trump translates to *Trumpet*

Trumpet sounds out "*45mph*"

Review

Fill in the Presidents (1 – 11)

W. H. Harrison, Van Buren, Polk, J. Q. Adams, Jefferson, J. Adams, Jackson, Washington, Monroe, Madison, Tyler

1. _____

2. _____

3. _____

4. _____

5. _____

6. _____

7. _____

8. _____

9. _____

10. _____

11. _____

Fill in the Presidents (12 – 22)

A. Johnson, Grant, Taylor, Arthur, Buchanan, Hayes,
Fillmore, Pierce, Cleveland, Lincoln, Coolidge

12. _____

13. _____

14. _____

15. _____

16. _____

17. _____

18. _____

19. _____

20. _____

21. _____

22. _____

Fill in the Presidents (23 – 26)

Cleveland, B. Harrison, McKinley, T. Roosevelt

23. _____

24. _____

25. _____

26. _____

Fill in the Presidents (27 – 45)

27. _____

28. _____

29. _____

30. _____

31. _____

32. _____

33. _____

34. _____

35. _____

36. _____

37. _____

38. _____

39. _____

40. _____

41. _____

42. _____

43. _____

44. _____

45. _____

Definitions

Below is a list of words and their definitions. To help you remember the definition, each word is slightly changed into a memorable phrase, which is <u>underlined</u>, making it easier to remember.

Assurance - A positive statement to give promise or confidence.
You <u>sure</u> need to <u>rinse</u> (assurance) if you want self-confidence.

Asylum - Protection or shelter from danger.
I have to <u>sigh</u> when a <u>limb</u> (asylum) is all the protection I need.

Auxiliary - Helping or giving assistance or support.
Many helpers gave me assistance to feed this <u>ox celery</u> (auxiliary).

Brevity - Short duration, brief time.
The <u>brave tea</u> (brevity) was just plain short.

Candid - Sincere, open.
Let me be frank and sincere about this. The <u>can did</u> (candid) have frankfurters inside.

Comport - To behave oneself in a particular manner.
The <u>computer</u> (comport) was well behaved.

Concise - Clear and succinct; expressed in few words.
When <u>Connie sighed</u> (concise), she expressed herself in few words.

Console - Comfort someone during time of disappointment or grief.
<u>Connie</u>'s <u>soul</u> (console) was very comforting.

Cubicle - Partitioned off compartment, small space.
<u>Cute bees who kill</u> (cubicle) are buzzing around the compartment.

Demure - Reserved and modest in behavior or manner.
<u>Da mirror</u> (demure) was very modest in its manner.

Depreciation - Loss or decrease in value.
CLUE: When you're <u>appreciated</u> your value is high; whereas when you're <u>depreciated</u> you're not highly regarded.

Deteriorate - Inferior in value or quality.
Since <u>Dee and Terry ate</u> (deteriorate), they're wearing away.

Dilate - Make wider or larger.
If your pupils <u>die late</u> (dilate), I can see more of your eyes.

Divulge - To reveal information not previously known.
Once you <u>die vulture</u> (divulge), I'm telling everyone.

Dross - Regarded as worthless or rubbish.
Miss <u>Dee Ross</u> (dross) is full of rubbish.

Drudgery - Dull or hard work
<u>R U</u> getting <u>D's</u> (drudgery)? You need hard, tiresome
work to get better. CLUE: there are *d's* on each side of *R U*.

Dwindle - Gradually diminishes in size.
<u>Da window</u> (dwindle) keeps diminishing in size.

Enlightened - To instruct or impart knowledge.
<u>EN-velopes and lights</u> (enlightened) impart a lot of knowledge.

Envoy - (*ON-Voy*) An accredited messenger or representative.
There's a messenger <u>ON</u> every <u>VOY</u>-age (envoy).

Escalate - Increase in intensity, magnitude.
Escalator (escalate) at the mall transports people upward at a very fast pace.

Expedite - An action or process accomplished quickly.
X's and P's that Date (expedite) need to leave the alphabet very quickly.

Feign = pronounced *fain*. Pretend an injury or feeling.
Don't pretend to faint (feign).

Flair - Having the ability to do something very well with style.
When you fly through the air (flair) you have a distinctive style and skill.

Flippant - Disrespectful attitude; not serious
His comment about wanting to flip ants (flippant) was not very serious.

Forestall - To delay by taking precautionary measures.
Clean the 4th stall (forestall) last. Prevent from doing it first.

Garble - Scrambled message or signal.
I could never get a good signal in the garbage (garble).

Grievous - Very severe or serious.
Feeling sorrow and pain because the gravy (grievous) is not here.

Heterogeneous - Process involving substances in different phases.
Those who heat their jeans (heterogeneous) go in different phases.

Horde - Large group of people.
Too many people are sitting on my horse (horde).

Immunity - Resisting toxins or disease.
Emma's new knee, dipped in tea (immunity), resisted diseases.

Impel - An urge or drive to do something.
Had an urge to drive my father's <u>Impala</u> (impel) car.

Incredulous - Unwilling to believe something.
I'm skeptical that my name is on that <u>cruddy</u> <u>list</u> (incredulous).

Inscribe - To write or carve words for permanent record.
While in <u>crib</u> (inscribe), I engraved and wrote.

Institute - Organization or society with a common factor,
especially scientific or educational.
<u>Stay in and</u> <u>toot</u> (institute) and be a part of this scientific facility.

Liability - A debt or financial obligation.
<u>If you lie to Bill</u> (liability) it will cost you.

Monologue - Mono means one. Mono-log. A long speech
by an actor. The lone actor gave a speech atop the <u>mono-log</u>

Preposterous - Absurd, ridiculous, not contrary to reason.
Are you saying this is a <u>purring poster</u> (preposterous)? No way!

Prognosis - A forecast of the likely course of an ailment or disease.
The <u>frog knows sis</u> (prognosis) that she will recover from her disease.

Proponent - One who supports an issue; an advocate.
The <u>pro poor ant</u> (proponent) always supports the cause.

Pugnacious - Quick to quarrel or argue.
<u>Pugs</u> in any <u>nation</u> (pugnacious) always want to argue.

Quaver - Involuntarily shake; quick, short movements.
CLUE: Write the word *quaver* on a piece of paper. Then, shake it.
You'll always remember its definition.

Rasping - An unpleasant or grating sound.
The <u>raspberry</u> (rasping) makes an unpleasant sound when plucked
from the vine

Realm - Domain or field of activity.
Only a <u>real elm</u> (realm) is in the field of study.

Recoil - To draw back.
CLUE: After you get up from a mattress those coils spring back.

Recoup - Reimburse, return as an equivalent.
After I lost the can of <u>soup</u> (recoup), I found another on my way home.

Rejuvenate - To make fresher, newer, feeling of youth.
If you <u>re-chew an ant</u> (rejuvenate), you'll feel young again.

Reek - Stench, bad odor.
The <u>creek</u> (reek) has an unpleasant smell.

Relentless - Persistent and steady.
Those who are persistent, <u>lend less</u> (relentless).

Remunerate - Pay for services done or rendered.
I pay only for <u>rims I knew</u> (remunerate).
CLUE: Note the word <u>rate</u> is in remune<u>rate</u>; as in pay a rate.

Rendering – drawing of a proposed structure.
<u>When do we ring</u> (rendering) the artist to draw the picture?

Repugnant - . Very distasteful.
The <u>pug and ant</u> (repugnant) were very offensive and disagreeable.

Rivulet - small stream or brook.
The <u>river you let</u> me use is a small stream.

Scuttle - Run hurriedly or quickly.
The <u>scooter</u> (scuttle) got here <u>quickly</u>.

Squander - To wastefully spend.
Each time he <u>squats under</u> (squander) the table he spends foolishly.

Staccato - Disconnected parts; abrupt.
When you <u>stack cars with toes</u> (staccato) you're disconnected and detached.

Statute - Established rule or law.
The guy who kept the <u>stat, shoots</u> (statute) at the rules. Doesn't he know it's the law?

Need a definition to remember?

For assistance, contact the author at <u>paul@mellormemory.com</u>, or visit his website at <u>www.mellormemory.com</u>.

Art

Painting: American Gothic
Artist: Grant Wood
Year: 1930

To remember the name of the painting, the artist, and year it was completed, ask yourself, *what do you already know about this painting?* We see a house in the background, while in the foreground is a woman and man. The man is holding a pitchfork. That is what we know.

Since that is what we know, we must connect the three things we want to know (painting, artist, and year) to what we already know. The painting is giving us an abundance of clues. We just have to find them.

Look at the roof line at the top of the house pictured directly in the center. What letter does that resemble? Do you see an *A*? Coincidently, *A* is the beginning letter to the painting's name.

Look at the woman's collar. What letter does that resemble? Do you see an *A*? It's the beginning letter to the painting's name. That helps in

73

remembering that it's *American Gothic*. The person on the left is a girl, true? There's another clue. **A G**irl. *A G* stands for American Gothic.

What do you think that grand home is made of? Could it be wood? That will help us to remember the artist is Grant Wood.

The foreground has three principles; the woman, the man, the pitchfork. Three represents 19<u>3</u>0.

How many prongs are on the pitchfork? There's another clue. And look, after the prongs you'll see the lens to the man's glasses. It looks a lot like a zero, as in <u>O</u>. Put the prongs and the lens together and you get 30; the year of the painting.

How many fingers do you see on the man's hand? Do you see three? And, notice how his fist is shaped like an <u>O</u> as he's holding the pitchfork. Put them together and what number do you have? That's right, it's 30; the year of the painting.

Painting: Whistler's Mother
Artist: James Whistler
Year: 1871

What do you already know about this painting? You know what the painting looks like. The rest is easy. Connect what you already know to what you're trying to remember; which is the year (1871) it was painted and the artist.

Doesn't the right-hand side of the curtain resemble a 1? Look at the picture on the wall. There's a frame within a frame. Count the borders of those frames and you'll come up with 8. Doesn't the top of her head down to her back resemble a 7? And look, there's only 1 leg of the chair visible. Put it all together and what do you have? That's right, 1871. The answer is right in front of you.

Her mouth is closed because jammed (James) down her throat is a whistle (Whistler).

Remember … connect what you want to know to what you DO know.

Painting: The Persistence of Memory
   Artist: Salvador Dali
    Year: 1931

The time pieces appear they are no longer ticking; or no longer purring. Purring sounds like <u>Pur-sistence</u>. Time is a distant <u>Memory</u>; The Persistence of Memory.

The time pieces are gently folded. There's only one letter in the alphabet that is gently folded; S. The letter S stands for *Salvador*. Times pieces that no longer operate cost less than a Dollar; similar to Dali. Also, note the second and third letters in both names are *a* and *l*.

Three (3) time pieces are folded, while one (1) isn't. The year is 1931.

Painting: Freedom from Want
Artist: Norman Rockwell
Year: 1943

A Free turkey. Want some? Freedom from Want.

The turkey is about to hit the table like a <u>rock</u> (Rockwell). It's <u>normal</u> (Norman) for Thanksgiving.

Look closely and count the faces of the men seated (4), and then count the faces of the women (3) seated. Put them together and you have the year of the painting (19<u>43</u>).

Painting: Christina's World
Artist: Andrew Wyeth
Year: 1948

Her hands and arms are positioned resembling the letter <u>C</u>. It's her <u>C</u> in <u>C</u>hristina's World.

Draw a straight line from her foot to her head. Then, a line from her head to each building, and instantly a huge letter *Y* appears. <u>Y</u> stands for <u>Y-eth</u>.

Christina's World is four (4) syllables, double that and you have the year of the painting (19<u>48</u>).

History from A - Z

Apollo 11. All A's with <u>A</u>pollo, <u>A</u>rmstrong, and <u>A</u>ldrin, as they enter the <u>C</u> (<u>C</u>ollins) of tranquility.
The two l's in Commander Co<u>ll</u>ins' name reminds us that it was Apollo 11. Also, Armstrong's famous words were, "<u>1</u> small step for man. <u>1</u> giant leap for mankind." 1 and 1 translates to 11.

Boston Massacre. March 5, 1770. Beginning with snowballs thrown by an angry mob, British soldiers <u>MARCH</u> in, use their <u>5</u> fingers to pick up their weapons, and shoot and kill many protestors. If only it were <u>70</u> degrees.

Cuban Missile Crisis. CASTING (Castro) a CUBE (Cuba) into the CAN (Kennedy) is bad luck (bad luck number 13; number of days). Americans RUSH (Russia) to form a blockade.
Note: Each word of <u>Cuban Missile Crisis</u> has <u>2</u> syllables. (196<u>2</u>).

D-Day. June 6, 1944. I'm SICK, SICK (6, 6) of this war continuing. I'm FOR, FOR (4, 4) the war ending. This will be a turning point. (06-06-44).

Emancipation Proclamation. Be FREE in Sixty-THREE. Lincoln issued proclamation on January 1, 1863.

French and Indian War. Imagine <u>FRENCH</u> toast going <u>IN</u> the <u>MIDDLE</u> of the toaster for your 17-year old Paris friend. The result is a Paris TREAT. (Paris Treaty in the mid 1700's).

Gold Rush. It was in 1849 where John <u>Sutter</u> discovered gold at his saw mill. <u>SUTT</u>ingly (Suddenly), the rush was on!

Hindenburg. Caught fire in May 1937 in Lakehurst, New Jersey.
It was Mayday when the disaster occurred. Using your fingers to count syllables in *Hin-den-burg* you show **3** fingers, while **7** are hidden. 19**37**. Many were hurt in Lake 'HURTS', NJ.

Industrial Revolution.   The machines, covered IN DUST (Industrial), need to start cranking to better impact the way we live.

Johnstown Flood. Water on top of water creates a flood. The word, J<u>o</u>hnst<u>o</u>wn on top of J<u>o</u>hnst<u>o</u>wn creates two 8's (88) represented by the letter o. The same applies by stacking the word, Fl<u>oo</u>d (88). Add one more number and stick a <u>fork</u> in it to remember the great flood happened in 1**889** when the South <u>Fork</u> Dam broke resulting in over 2000 lost lives.

King, **Martin Luther**, Civil Rights leader. Assassinated on April 4, 1968 in Memphis.
4 letters in K-I-N-G, died 4th month and 4th day of year. Add those two 4's to get **8**, for 196**8**. **Mem**phis is where **M**urderer **E**nded **M**artin's life.

Louisiana **Purchase**. **8** letters in P-U-R-C-H-A-S-E represents over **8**00,000 square miles of land acquired in the early 1**8**00's.

Mayflower. The English ship arrived in the New World in 1**6**2**0**. HINT: **6** letters in 'flower.' **2** words; May Flower. The letter **0** looks like an ocean.

New Deal. You Rose (Roosevelt) to deal (New Deal) new cards out evenly; 3 to you and 3 to me making 6 cards (1933-1936). Then, you SEW (as in SOCIAL Programs) the cards together.

Oregon Trail. I, I KNOW I'M in over my head walking the Oregon Trail, which reminds us that the states included to covering the TRAIL were… Illinois, Iowa, Kansas, Nebraska, Oregon, Wyoming, Idaho, and Missouri.

Panama Canal. 1 DOOR (rhymes with 4) opened in '14 for giving ships a shortcut to go from ocean to ocean. (1914).

Quakers. While walking down the road (Rhode Island), you pull out a pencil (Pennsylvania) from your new jersey (NJ) when suddenly an earthquake shakes you to the way of the Lord. You are safe. In 17th century America, you go where you are tolerated.

Rough Riders. The R's have it with Theodore Roosevelt and his Rough Riders, who during the Spanish-American War, captured the sought-after locale of San Juan Hill. *Juanna know more?* Visit your local library.

Stamp Act of 1765. Visualize a colony (Colonists) of stamps about to soak up the spilled INK (for England) on all printed paper material. It will be very taxing (tax) on everyone. The countdown begins … 7, 6, 5, (1765).

Trail of Tears. To all the Indiana Tribes affected: Don't be Chicken (*Chickasaw*), just put on your Poncho (*Ponca*), grab your Musket (*Muscogee*) and a Chockful (*Choctaw*) of Cherries (*Cherokee*) and get in your Semi (*Seminole*) and go west.

Uncle Tom's Cabin. … *Tom's* …Take that letter *s* and place it in front of the *T*. Next, turn the *m* upside down and you have the name of the author (Stowe) who wrote one of America's best-selling novels.

To remember the main characters, visualize Art-work (Arthur) on Shells (Shelby) sandwiched around a Tom-ato (Tom), making for a nice Meal (Emily).

To recall the publication date (1852), notice how the *s* in Tom'**s**, resembles a 5 which is situated between the 2 words of *Tom* and *Cabin* (1852). Also, there are 5 characters in each set of words (U-N-C-L-E, T-O-M-'-S, and C-A-B-I-N). Choose one of those words and you have 2 left over.

Voyagers. The SODA (de Soto) hit the FLOOR (Florida). The GAME (de Gama) is being played so put me IN (India). MA, GEL (Magellan) is what I need to navigate the earth.

Whiskey Rebellion. Visualize stirring whiskey with pencils, and you'll know that it was in Pennsylvania where the uprising began to protest the country's first imposed domestic product tax. Prior to taxing DISTILLED spirits, things were STILL.

X marks the spot - Are you where you want to be? You have the power to start making History.

Yorktown. Two O's in Yorktown is the clue that it was October, which any 19-year older can tell you, when Cornwallis surrendered to Washington. It was such a great day that folks 8 (ate) 1 (one) York Peppermint Patty. (October 19, 1781).

Zion. Zion National Park is one of over 50 national parks in the United States. It's so GREAT that it sits between a GRAND ROCK that YOU can see this summer. Top 5 most visited parks: GREAT Smoky, GRAND Canyon, ZION, ROCKY Mountain, and YOSEMITE.

Remembering the Gettysburg Address

W alk up the steps to the Lincoln Memorial in Washington D.C. and you'll notice many heads facing to the left. Yes, the visitors have already seen the imposing figure sitting in the chair, but it's the words to this man's speech they want to see.

Two-hundred seventy-two (272) words, engraved onto the wall at the Memorial, were first spoken on a Pennsylvania battlefield on November 19, 1863. Those words not only instilled confidence to Lincoln's fighting cavalry, but also instilled in them that their sweat and blood was greatly appreciated. The words galvanized our nation to always remember the strength and will for those who lost their lives fighting in a worthy and mighty cause.

The Gettysburg Address, whose originator of the message said, ...*the world will little note, nor long remember what we say here...*' was so wrong. Lincoln's words have lived on. Perhaps you have given the address, as well.

Whether it's the Gettysburg Address, a class speech, or a school play, there are methods in remembering the words. The key is associating what you know to what you're trying to memorize.

Four score and seven years ago our fathers brought forth on this continent, a new nation, conceived in Liberty, and dedicated to the proposition that all men are created equal.

Now we are engaged in a great civil war, testing whether that nation, or any nation so conceived and so dedicated, can long endure.

Note the pattern in the first sentence with the word *four*. There's 4 score and brought 4th. That's memorable. How can we remember *conceived* and *dedicate*? Conceive is a beginning, while DEAD-icate is an ending. That's a memorable pattern.

How can we remember *created equal* to *Now, we are engaged..*? Think of equal rights. The National Organization for Women (NOW) stands for equal rights. *Equal rights* to *NOW* is a memorable connection, especially when you're married or *engaged*. Then, you hope you don't get into a *great civil war* with your partner.

We are met on a great battlefield of that war. We have come to dedicate a portion of that field, as a final resting place for those who here gave their lives that that nation might live. It is altogether fitting and proper that we should do this.

Notice the first two sentences begin with same word; *We.* In the first sentence, two 3-letter words follow (are met). The next sentence, it's two 4-letter words (have come).
The keys words are 'dedicate and final'. May be easier to remember if we say '<u>dead</u>-icate and <u>final</u>.

It is altogether FITTING. Fitting begins with F, same letter that begins the word, FINAL. Also, Lincolns talks about <u>P</u>ORTION of that <u>F</u>IELD. Reverse the P F to F P to remind you it's <u>F</u>ITTING and <u>P</u>ROPER.

But, in a larger sense, we can not dedicate -- we can not consecrate -- we can not hallow -- this ground. The brave men, living and dead, who struggled here, have consecrated it, far above our poor power to add or detract.

Key words are '**d**edicate', '**c**onsecrate' and '**hall**ow'. Think of the President in **D**. **C**. walking the **hall**owed halls. Notice the contradictions; there's living and dead, and add and detract.

The world will little note, nor long remember what we say here, but it can never forget what they did here. It is for us the living, rather, to be dedicated here to the unfinished work which they who fought here have thus far so nobly advanced.

Rhythm of the 'n' words' of note, nor, and never, as well as uNfinished and nobly.

It is rather for us to be here dedicated to the great task remaining before us -- that from these honored dead we take increased devotion to that cause for which they gave the last full measure of devotion -- that we here highly resolve that these dead shall not have died in vain --

… dedicated to the GREAT task REmaining.
Letter after G in 'great', is RE, which are the leading letters for Remaining.

Key words are 'honored dead' and 'increased devotion'. In the alphabet, H comes before I (honored / increased). Words *dead* and *devotion* begin with letter *d*.

Note the pattern of those *d* words: dedicated, dead, devotion, devotion, dead, died.

... that this nation, under God, shall have a new birth of freedom -- and that government of the people, by the people, for the people, shall not perish from the earth.

Key words are Government of, by, for, perish.

The second letter of *Government* is the beginning of the next word; *of*.

The sentence follows with *by* and then *for*. Remember that 2 comes before 3 and 4. *By* has 2 letters and *for* has 3 letters.

10 Guidelines for Giving a *Successful* Speech

10. Have confidence that you can do this. Never second-guess yourself. Remember, you're relaying information. Think about the people in the audience who will learn something from you. What a privilege it is to be able to share that message.

9. The audience is rooting for you. They want you to succeed. Unlike stepping into enemy territory as a visiting quarterback where you're physically being attacked and booed, audiences are always pulling for the speaker.

8. Be authentic. You're one of a kind. Show your true personality.

7. When introduced, stand before the audience without saying a word. Count to three before beginning your speech. Let the audience get adjusted in their seats so they'll be ready to hear you. Avoid saying your first word as you're turning to face the audience.

6. Avoid memorizing your speech word-for-word. Instead, link one idea into another. Be conversational. You don't memorize your phone calls to your friends, do you?

5. Practice your speech at home with the written words on a table. If you forget, avoid the temptation to look at your notes. This is good practice getting through your speech if you're forgetting during your big moment.

4. If you're memorizing a long quote or Gettysburg Address, practice by dividing the speech into sections. Use gestures while saying words softly and loudly, like a rhythm of a dance, this helps in remembering.

3. Link a part of your speech that you know to what you don't know. Search for patterns to bridge that gap. Practice again.

2. Go to a busy fast-food restaurant and stand in line. Mentally give the speech while looking at people in front of you. This prepares you for standing in front of others. Gauge how you feel. You're standing amongst people and you are mentally giving your talk.

1. Surveys tell us that public speaking is the #1 fear, but look at you. You're overcoming this fear by delivering a powerful presentation which many people wouldn't dare to take on. Congratulations. You're a leader.

Spelling

To paraphrase Marilyn vos Savant, *Guinness Book of World Record* holder as having the highest IQ, there is no way you can identify the intelligence level of a good speller, however, it does raise the question when you see the writings of a bad speller.

Deer Mom,
Remember when ewe said eye kneaded two practice my spelling? Well, my knew computer will dew it fore me. When eye misspell a word the computer tells me sew. It's grate too sea technology key ping pace and knot passing us bye.
Sin celery,
Your loving sun

It's no wonder why people don't like to write; we can't spell! And, if we can make shortcuts to correct spelling, we'll take that option every time. Go ahead, text yur bff on that 1.

This section helps you get it correct each time by putting clues into each sentence of the 1001 frequently misspelled words. Each sentence contains words or letters in **BOLD** to help you lock in the correct spelling.

As an example, you're not sure on the correct spelling of the word *vitamin*. Is it *vitemin* with an *e*, or *vitaman* with an *a*? And, is it vita-*man* or *min*? By associating the **BOLD** letters to the word, you can't go wrong.

Vitamin – **Am I** supposed to take a vit**ami**n? Also, we can say that **it** helps to take v**it**amins. This tells us the word *vitamin* is spelled with a *T* not a *D*, as in *vidamin*.

I can also mean *eye*, as in … an injured *I* (eye) can *handicap* you. This aids us to remember that *hand**i**cap* is spelled with an *i*, instead of an *a* or an *e*.

Other codes we need to know.

The words *you* and *see* are coded to *U* and *C*. For example, **U C e**very drip from the fa**uce**t or **U** and **me** create a loud vol**ume**. Do *U C* what I mean?

The word *are* codes to *r*, as in **U r** abs**ur**d.

CT is coded to Connecticut, as in … citizens of **CT** have a Yankee diale**ct**.

CC codes to credit card, as in … pay bro**cc**oli on your **cc**.

ER is emergency room, as in … flatt**er**y in the **ER** won't work.

ERA is Equal Rights Amendment, as in … I **fed** the **ERA** in **federa**l court.

On the following pages you'll find 1001 frequently misspelled words. The stories behind them, with the help of the **bold** letters, make the spelling of these words memorable. So, if you're one who takes an **oath** to l**oath**e, puts **gel** on ba**gel**s, or if **I c u r** getting a mani**cur**e, enjoy this section and spell it right.

aardvark	2 **A**'s, on **aardvark**, ran down **rd** to the **ark**
abandon	don't **abandon a band on** my finger
abdomen	**do men** have big ab**domen**s
abscess	**s**ore **c**ut will become an ab**sc**ess
absolutely	**so** should **U** **e**at? Ab**solu**tely
absurd	**u r** abs**ur**d
abyss	**Y** must you put me in this ab**y**ss
accelerate	2 **C**'s are a**cc**elerating
accidentally	2 **C**'s a**cc**iden**tally** collide. **Tally** up damage
acclimate	**c climate** change and a**cclimate** yourself
accommodate	a**ccommo**date 2 **C**'s, **O**'s and **M**'s
accuracy	if your a**ccura**cy is off you get **3 C**'s
achieve	**I** ach**ieve** in the **eve**ning
acquaintance	an acquain**tan**ce gets a **tan**
acquisition	**U** and **I** will **sit** after the acq**uisit**ion
acrobat	**c** an a**crob**atic **rob**ber
adequate	**A** grade of **D** does not **equate adequate**ly
adjourn	**D J** ad**journ**s the meeting
administrator	administrat**o**r's door is **o**pen
admittance	**tan mitt** has gained ad**mittan**ce
adolescence	**E**! Don't pick **Dole** pineapple in a**dole**sc**e**nce
aeronautics	vowels **a**, **e**, **o**, **u** are **aeronauti**c, not **I**
affect	achieving an **A** **a**ffects my **a**ttitude
affidavit	**f**ist hit **f**ace. **2** black **I's** and an a**ffidavit**
aggravate	**G**'s are a**gg**ravating
allegiance	**GI a**lways pledges alle**gia**nce to the flag
allowance	**all** are entitled to an **all**owance
ambassador	am**bass**ad**o**r has a mouth like a **bass**; **o**pen
ancient	**C, I** am not an**ci**ent
anecdote	an a**nec**dote about **nec**tarine
annihilate	**Hi, Ann** and **I** are **late**, so don't **annihilate** us
anniversary	**Ann** and **I** are **ver**y **ha**ppy on our **anniversary**
anonymous	**no NY mous**e made a**nonymous** call

93

apostrophe	every apos**trophe** deserves a **troph**y
appearance	2 **P**'s **ran** on stage to make an a**PP**ea**RAN**ce
architect	Gateway **Arch** was built by an **arch**itect
artillery	**tiller** in ar**tiller**y
ascend	**SC** (South Carolina) will a**SC**end
assurance	I **a**ssure you assur**a**nce is spelled with an **A**
asthma	give me **the** medicine **Ma**. I have as**thma**
asylum	**Y** don't **u** go to the as**y**l**u**m
avalanche	**C, he** told us an avalan**che** was coming
bachelor	**ache** to be a b**ache**lor
bagel	put **gel** on your ba**gel**
ballad	**Al**, a young **lad**, sang a b**allad**
banana	**Nana** ate ba**nana**
bankrupt	**U PT** (point) me to the bank. I'm bankr**upt**
baptize	catching my **z**'s waiting to be bapti**z**ed
barbecue	**be** ready to **cue** me to bar**becue**
barricade	**BA! RR! I** am **barri**cading sheep and lions
battalion	**bat ta lion** with **battalion**
battery	a batt**er**y will send you to the **ER**
beautiful	**Bea, u** are **beau**tiful
behavior	all vowels, except U, have good b**e**h**a**v**io**r
beige	**be** b**e**ige and no one will notice
believe	never be**lie**ve a **lie**
belligerent	**E**'s are b**e**llig**e**r**e**nt
beneficial	ben**e**ficial to be h**e**lpful
benign	**G**, you're very beni**gn**
bequeath	I bequ**eat**h you to **eat**
binoculars	**no c** without bi**noc**ulars
boisterous	h**oist** b**oist**erous boys away
bonnet	**on** the **net** is your b**onnet**
boulevard	**y**u**le**tide on bo**ule**vard
boundary	bound**a**ry of alphabet is from **a** to z
bouquet	**o u** do deserve this b**ou**quet

94

bracelet	**brace** her and **let** her keep **bracelet**
brilliant	the **I** of the **ant** is brill**iant**
broccoli	pay bro**cc**oli on your **cc** (credit card)
bulletin	a **bullet** hit the **bulletin** board
bungalow	my **gal** is in the bun**gal**ow
burial	bur**ial** of **Al**
cabinet	look **in** cab**in**et
caffeine	**in** the **cafe** I like my **caffein**e with an added **f**
calcium	**C, I** drink milk - y**um**! Good cal**cium**
calendar	**A**ugust is on the calend**ar**
caliber	**I** have the cal**i**ber to succeed
calisthenics	**is the** cal**isthe**nics program scheduled today
camaraderie	3 **A**'s have great c**a**m**a**r**a**derie in **Erie**, PA
camouflage	**mou**se was ca**mouflag**ed and **flag**ged me down
capital	visit **a** state capit**a**l city
capitol	dome in Capit**ol** looks like this: **O**
caramel	**ram** car**am**el down your throat
carbohydrate	**Y** are carboh**y**drates good for you
career	**e**lementary **e**ducation is an excellent car**ee**r
Caribbean	**bean**s in the Ca**ribbean** stick to my **rib**
cartilage	**I lag** behind with my bad cart**ilag**e
cashmere	**me** pay **cash** for this **cashme**re
casserole	the **role** of **Cass** is to make **e**very **casserole**
casualty	**Su** (sue) **Al** for your ca**sual**ty
category	I **ate** every c**ate**gory of food
caterpillar	take **pill** to see a **caterpillar cater** p**ar**ty
caulk	cau**l**k the e**L**ephant
cauliflower	**I** h**aul cauliflower** to **flower** market
cavalier	**Val** and **I** were ca**vali**er about it
ceiling	**I**'s are holding up **L** in ce**il**ing
celebrate	**ele**phant c**eleb**rates
cemetery	**E**'s are in c**e**m**e**t**e**ry
ceremony	**E**veryone was at the cer**e**mony

channel	**1 L** = **1** channe**l**
chaos	**cha**nge this **cha**os
chasm	**has** everyone seen this c**has**m
chauffeur	chau**ffeur** **F**red **f**erries **e**ach **u**ncle **r**eligiously
chocolate	**O** how I love ch**ocolate late** at night
chrysanthemum	**the mum** is in the chrysan**themum**
Cincinnati	**in** the **Inn** in C**incinn**ati one at a **ti**me
cinnamon	at the **Inn** the c**inn**amon cost **mon**ey
coincidence	my **den** is like yours. What a coinci**den**ce
collision	2 **L**'s had a co**ll**ision
colossal	**Co** can't afford **loss** of **Al**. It would be **colossal**
column	**Um, n** by the way, the col**umn** is in my way
commemorate	**memo** is sent to co**mmemo**rate new **3M** office
commensurate	the **mens u rate** com**mensurate**
commission	2 **o**'s, **i**'s, **m**'s and **s**'s have received c**ommissio**n
committed	2 **m**'s and **t**'s are co**mmitt**ed to each other
compelled	com**pell**ed to ask for a **Pell** Grant
competent	**pets** are not com**petent** to **ent**er school
compliance	compli**a**nce states that alphabet begins with **a**
conceive	conce**ive** with an **I V**
conscience	**science** says that **con**men have no **conscience**
contemplate	con**template** firing **temp** since he was **late**
continent	giant **tin** **ent**ers a con**tin**ent
controversy	contr**over**sy is **over**
counselor	if you get an **O** on your paper see counsel**O**r
credence	cre**den**ce of that is in my **den**
credulous	**o u** are credul**ou**s, aren't you
criticize	I will crit**ici**ze when **I c** him catch **z**'s
culinary	**a**pron is worn by all culin**a**ry students
cupboard	**cup** on **board** is in **cupboard**
curiosity	I have a cu**riosit**y to **sit** in **Rio**
Czar	**C** the **C**zar
Czechoslovakia	**c z echo** in **Czecho**slovakia

96

dangerous	danger**o**us! **O** people allowed in
dandelion	**lion** stepped on dande**lion**
debris	deb**ris is** on road
deceit	**c** between the **e**'s not to dec**e**it
decimal	**I'm a** small dec**ima**l mark
decision	**dec**ision of the **dec**ade
dedicate	**I** ded**i**cate this building
deferred	**deferred** is when you **defer** to paint it **red**
defiance	d**ance** has defi**ance**
definitely	it's def**inite**ly **nite**time
deliberate	**be** delib**e**rate
delicatessen	**ate s**alty **s**andwich **en**tering delic**atessen**
delicious	**I c iou** for this del**iciou**s meal
delinquent	delinqu**ent ent**ers Principal's office
dependent	d**e**p**e**nd**e**nt on **e**'s to spell this word
desperate	with **ESP** I'd be d**espera**te about the **ERA**
despicable	I have **ESP** about that d**esp**i**cable cable** bill
deteriorate	deteri**o**rate the **O** in deteri**o**rate
devastate	floods can dev**astate a state**
devious	**IOU** for being dev**iou**s
dialect	residents of **CT** have a Yankee diale**ct**
diaper	**ape** wore a di**ape**r
dictionary	diction**a**ry starts with letter **A**
difference	no di**ff**erence between **F**rank and **F**rancis
dilemma	**I Emma** have a di**lemma**
diligent	**I I** sir, I will be a more d**i**l**igent gent**leman
dining	**in** the d**in**ing room
disastrous	**di** (die) if **Astro**naut missions are **disastrous**
discrepancy	**is** there a discre**pan**cy with this **pan**
discussion	**is cuss**ing a problem? Let's have a d**iscuss**ion
disease	a **dis ease** may cause a **disease**
distance	I saw her **tan** at a dis**tan**ce
dominant	that is one domin**ant ant**

dominion	**mini** do**mini**on
dormant	**ant** in my **dorm** is **dormant**
drudgery	**e**very job has its drudg**e**ry
dubious	du**bio**us **bio** on **us**
duplicate	**up** came a d**up**licate
eaves	l**eaves** falling on **eaves**
eccentric	**CC**'s make you e**ccen**tric without a **cent**
effervescent	**f**ossil **f**uel in **RV** creates ef**ferve**scent **scent**
efficiency	**I c I** live in an ef**fici**ency apartment
Eisenhower	**e**xcellent **I**ke was **Ei**senhower
elaborate	please, e**labor**ate on her **labor**
electricity	electri**city** reaches each **city**
elegant	**leg** of an **ant** is e**legant**
elementary	**men** in **tar** are at **elementar**y school
elicit	**c** me between the **I**'s; give me an el**ici**t response
eligible	el**igi**ble bachelor has nice **I**'s
eliminate	you have one **min**ute to eli**mina**te
ellipse	el**e**phant **lips** on the **ellips**e
eloquent	**O E**! She's el**o**qu**e**nt
emanate	after **man ate** he was able to e**manate**
embarrassed	**Barr**y **embarr**assed **me** (*me* backward is *em*)
employee	3 **E**'s are **e**mploy**e**d to spell *Employ**ee***
enchant	**e**agles are **e**nchanting
encourage	**en**tertainers who have **courage encourage**
encroach	**roach en**croach**ed by en**tering room
encyclopedia	**en**joy the **en**cyclopedia
endeavor	my d**ear**, don't **end endea**vor
endowment	**end** of **men** is **end**ow**men**t
endurance	at the **end** he **ran** showing his **endura**nce
enforce	**en**forcers **en**ter building
engagement	**en**ter **en**gagement
engrave	**en**ter **grave** and **engrave**
enjoyment	**en**tertainment was pure **en**joyment

98

enlighten	**en**tering a room with **light** is **enlight**ening
enormous	**Norm**, the m**ouse** was e**normous**
envious	**IOU'S** are env**ious**
environment	**Ron**'s **men** are into the envi**ronmen**t
epidemic	epi**d**emic is coming. (**IE**. Stay indoors)
equilibrium	**I, I, I** …am losing my equi**li**br**i**um
equivalent	**Vale** is equi**vale**nt to a see-through mask
erroneous	**erron**eous contains **one err**or
escalator	there's a g**ator** on escal**ator**
essay	a **S**hort **S**tory is an e**ss**ay
estimate	at **e**leven o'clock I **estimate Tim ate**
etiquette	**Ti**me! **T**able **t**alk is not good e**ti**que**tt**e
evidence	evi**denc**e is in **den, C**
exaggerate	ex**agge**rate your **ag(g)e** by an extra **g**
exasperate	**Aspe**n, Colorado is ex**aspe**rating
exhilarate	ex**hilarate** is saying **hi** to an **LA rate**
existence	**is ten** in ex**isten**ce
experience	exp**eri**ence **Eric**, PA
explicit	expl**icit**? I know it when **I c it**
extemporaneous	**ex** Ford **Tempo ran** on **E extemporane**ously
extinct	**tin** cans are ex**tinct** in **CT** (Connecticut)
extraordinary	being extra ordinary is extraordinary
extravagant	the **ant** is extrav**ant**
fable	I'm **able** to tell a f**able**
fabulous	**u Lou** are fab**ulou**s
facade	**cade**t is showing a fa**cade**
facilitate	**c**, **I** let **it ate** therefore, I fa**cilitate**
facsimile	**s**end this fac**simile 1** (1 = I) **mile**
familiar	fami**liar liar**
fascinate	**S**outh **C**arolina **In**dustries fa**scin**ate me
fatigue	**g, u** look fati**gu**ed
faucet	**u c e**very drip from fa**uce**t
favorable	an able favor is favorable

99

feasible	**sib**lings are fea**sib**le
February	hot "**Bru**" in Fe**bru**ary
federal	I **fed** the **ERA** in **federa**l court
feign	**f**alse **e**vidence **i**nvolving **gn**ats is f**eign**ing
ferocious	an **O** made me fer**ociou**s. **C, IOU**
fiasco	**I, as co**-conspirator made a f**iasco** of things
fidelity	**f**armer **in deli** banks at **Fideli**ty
fierce	**fi**re is **fi**erce
finance	I had to fin**ance** the d**ance** lesson
flattery	flatt**er**y in the **ER** won't work
fluent	**flu ent**ers my mouth when I speak **fluent**ly
fluorescent	The **flu**, **ore**, and **scent** are **fluorescent**
foliage	**l**eaf **i**ncredibly **age**s during fo**liage** season
foreign	**reign**ing emperor is fo**reign**
formidable	to **form Ida** is **formida**ble
fragrance	I **ran** from the frag**ran**ce
frequency	"**Que**" the fre**que**ncy
frivolous	**RI** (Rhode Island) **vol**unteer is f**rivol**ous
fundamental	**fund**ing **a mental** program is **fundamental**
funeral	**fun** at **Al**'s **fun**eral
furious	**fur**, with an **IOU**, is **furiou**s
fuselage	If you **fuse** a **fuse**lage it will **age**
galaxy	**gal** with **ax** is in **galax**y
gallant	**all ant**s are g**allant**
gallery	**all** of the g**aller**y is in **ER**
gardener	there's a gar**den**er in my **den**
gaudy	**aud**ience is g**aud**y
gauge	**A U**, between the **G**'s, what's the **gaug**e
generous	**Gene** is **gene**rous
genius	**i**ntellectual **u**nder**s**tudy is a gen**ius**
genuine	hey, **u in** there, are you gen**uin**e
gesture	**est**imated time to ge**st**ure is anytime
geyser	ge**yse**r put an **s** into my **eye**

100

glamorous	the model, named **Mo Ro**, is gla**moro**us
glossary	gloss**a**ry is in **a** book
gorgeous	**Geo** was once a gor**geo**us car
government	**men govern** in **Governmen**t
governor	**Governor** will **govern**s **or** else
graceful	she was g**race**ful during **race**
gracious	**IOU** to be grac**iou**s
grammar	correct gr**a**mm**a**r earns you an **A**
granddaughter	**d**elightful **d**aughter is my gran**dd**aughter
gravity	if it falls **it**'s grav**it**y
greyhound	**e**xtra fast **hound** is a gr**ey**h**ound**
grievance	a lot of griev**ance** at the d**ance**
grieve	to cry (**ie**. gr**ie**ve)
grimace	sprayed by **mace** makes me gri**mace**
grocery	**e**verything is on groc**e**ry list
grotesque	**OT** at **Esqu**ire magazine is gr**otesqu**e
gruesome	color bl**ue** is gr**ue**some
guarantee	did he gua**rantee** he **ran** to the **tee**
guidance	**Dan** needs gui**dan**ce
guitar	**U** and **I** play g**uitar** in **tar**
gullible	the **gull I** see is g**ulli**ble
gymnasium	**as I** …**um** … said, I'm in the gymn**asium**
gypsum	**y p** on the **sum** total of g**ypsum**
Halloween	**hallow** halls of **Halloween**
hallucinate	**hall u c in** is where I **hallucin**ate
halo	Mr. **Hal O** is wearing a **halo**
halves	**Al ve**ry often wants h**alve**s
hamlet	**let** the **ham** into the **hamlet**
handicap	injured **I** can hand**i**cap you
handkerchief	**hand** Chief **Ker** a **handkerchief**
handle	can you h**andle** c**andle**
happily	I will l**i**ve happ**i**ly
harass	any donkey or **ass** will har**ass**

harbor	har**bor** is a **bore**
hardening	har**den**ing of the arteries occurs in the **den**
harmonious	**Harmon**, **IOU** to be **harmoniou**s
harness	harn**e**ss **e**very horse
hasten	**ha**! **Ten** horses couldn't **ha**s**ten** me
hatchet	**Chet**, with the **hat**, put down **hatchet**
haunt	my **aunt**'s house is **haunt**ed
haven	**aven**ue is a h**aven**
Hawaii	**I I** sir…send me to Hawa**ii**
hazard	avoid a h**azard**. Spell h**azard** with an **A**
hazel	**el**ephant has haz**el** eyes
headache	**a che**w! I have a head**ache**
heaven	don't l**eave** h**eaven**
hectic	**c**-ing the clock **tic** is he**ctic**
hedge	on the **edge** of a h**edge**
height	**he** has a lot of **he**ight to him
heirloom	**he** and **I** found the **hei**rloom
helicopter	**he** l**i**ves in a **heli**copter
helmet	ball **met** my hel**met**
hemisphere	**hem is** in **hemis**phere
heredity	**her edit** is **heredity**
heritage	when **it age**s it creates a her**itage**
hermitage	**it age**s in herm**itage**
hiatus	it's a **hiatus** if you don't say **hi at us**
hibernate	bear had to hib**er**nate in the **ER**
hideous	that's a **hideou**s **hideou**t
hierarchy	**hie**arch**y** in the **ER**, says the **arch**
hilarious	**hi Lar**ry, **IOU** money. You're **hilariou**s
hindrance	be**hind** him I **ran**. It was a **hindran**ce
hippopotamus	hippopo**tam**us was **tam**e
hoax	**Ho, Ho, Ho**! The **Ax** in the tree is a **hoax**
holiday	put a **lid** on your work during the ho**lid**ay
homicide	**I c I** favor the police on a hom**ici**de

honest	**Ho**! There's a **nest** in the chimney. **Honest**
horrible	The **rib** was hor**rib**le
horrified	**OR** and **RI** (Oregon/Rhode Island) h**orri**fied me
horticulture	**Ho**! The **RT** (root) **I c** is part of a **horti**culture
humor	hum**or** me **or** else
humorous	**o u** are humor**ou**s, aren't you
hungry	**ungr**ateful are not the h**ungr**y
hurricane	**hurr**y **I** see a **cane** in the **hurricane**
hustle	don't **st**op, hu**st**le
hydraulic	**y** did **u lic**k the hy**draulic** system
hydrogen	hydro**gen** is **gen**tle
hygiene	hyg**ie**ne (**ie**. Brush your teeth)
hypnotist	**y p** since **no** h**ypno**tist can h**ypno**tize me
hysteria	**y** all the h**yster**ia in the **ER**
iodine	**O**! I**o**dine hurts
icing	**c** the **ic**ing between your **I**'s
ideal	when **I deal** cards it's **ideal**
identical	**i c** you have identi**cal** twins
ideology	**idea** spelled with an **O** is a strange **ideo**logy
idiom	**id**iom has its own **ID**
idiot	**id**iot has an **ID**
idyllic	**y** are you id**y**llic
ignorant	**ant** is ignor**ant**
illegal	doing something **ill**egal makes me **ill**
illegible	**gible**t is ille**gible**
illicit	**3 I**'s are very ill**ic**it
Illinois	Illi**nois** is **nois**y
illiterate	if you're **illit**erate, **it** makes me **ill**
illuminate	**ill**umination makes me **ill**
illusion	both **ill**, two of **us**, are an **illus**ion
imagine	**imagin**e **I'm ag**ing
imbecile	**bec**ause **I'm** an **imbe**cile
imitation	**I'm it**, there's no **imit**ation

immaculate	**I'm** a **Ma** who is **imma**culate
immature	**I'm mature**, not **immature**
immigrant	**I grant** the imm**igrant** to enter
immune	**M&M**'s make you i**mm**une
impeccable	my talking cable says, **I'm** an **im**pec**cable cable**
implement	**ple**a is to im**ple**ment
importance	**I'm** of **imp**ort**a**nce who deserves an **A**
impress	**I'm press**ing to **impress** you
improvement	**prove** to me your im**prove**ment
inaccurate	**ACC** (Atl Coast Conf.) **u rate** is in**accurate**
inappropriate	if you **ate** an **app**le it's in**app**ropri**ate**
inaugurate	**2 of u** came **in** for the **In**a**ugu**ration
incentive	there's an in**cent**ive to pay a **cent**
incorporate	are you feeling **por** (poor) to incor**por**ate
incredible	color **red** is in**cred**ible
incumbent	**in**cumbent was voted **in**
indecent	1 **cent** was indecent
indefensible	**sibl**ings are indefen**sible**
indelible	**I** am indel**i**ble
independent	**pen** in **den** is inde**pendent**
index	ind**ex** is near the **ex**it
indictment	indi**ct**ment in **CT** (Connecticut)
indigenous	it's in**dig**enous to **dig**
individual	**dual** between two indivi**dual**s
industrial	indus**trial** man was on **trial**
inefficient	an **I** in a **cent** is ineffi**cient**
inevitable	it was inev**itable** that **I** sat at **table**
infamous	the **famous** are in**famous**
infant	**ant** is an inf**ant**
infirmary	please con**firm** that **Mary** is in the in**firmary**
inflammable	**M&M**'s are **able** to be infla**mmable**
inflation	in**flat**ion is **flat**
influence	b**lue** g**lue** will in**flue**nce you

104

ingredient	adding wrong ingre**die**nt may cause you to **die**
inhabitant	**habit** of an **ant** is being an in**habitant**
inhibition	hey **4 I**'s what's your in**hibiti**on?
inherit	I'd like to in**herit her IT**
initial	please in**iti**al my **3 I**'s
initiative	take the in**itiativ**e to get **4 I**'s
injustice	**just ice** is an in**justice**
innocence	**inn** by the **c**'s has an **inn**o**cen**ce
inspiration	**pirate** had ins**pirat**ion
instantaneous	the **instant an E O**pens **us**, it's **instantaneous**
instrument	**u men** play an instr**umen**t
intelligence	**gen**tlemen have intelli**gen**ce
intercede	inte**rc**ede by an **RC** Cola
intermittent	**tent** is on my intermit**tent** wipers
interrupt	inte**rr**upted at the **RR** tracks
intoxicate	call t**axi** if you're int**oxi**cated
intrigue	**g**, you intri**g**ue me
invigorate	**in or** out of pool and you'll feel **in**vig**or**ated
irregular	**i**s **R**oger **R**abbit **irr**egular
irresistible	**I** am irresist**i**ble
irresponsible	**I** respond when you're irresponsi**i**ble
irrevocable	**o** the **cable**, is that irrev**ocable**
Israel	**is Rae** in **Israe**l
itch	**it it**ches
jackal	two **Jackals** are named **Jack** and **Al**
jacket	**E T** always wears a jack**et**
jaguar	**g**, **u ar**e a big ja**guar**
jalopy	**Al** drove j**al**opy
janitor	janit**or** cleans toilet bowl shaped like an **O**
January	Janu**a**ry is first month. **A** is first letter
Japanese	Jap**ane**se story on **A 'n' E** television
jealous	**o u** are jeal**ou**s, aren't you?
jeopardy	got a **D** on Jeopa**rd**y

jersey	New J**ers**e**y** is on **E**ast Coast
jewelry	jewel**ry** was in **ry**e bread
jewels	**we** love je**we**ls
journey	**our** j**our**ney was exciting
jovial	I was jov**ial** to find radio d**ial**
joyous	**o** we are joy**o**us
journal	wrote in **our** j**our**nal
jubilant	**ant** and **I** were jub**i**l**ant**
jubilee	**Lee** was at jubi**lee**
judge	**Jud** is **Jud**ge
judgment	**g**, **men** are jud**gmen**tal
judiciary	**I c I** am on jud**ici**ary committee
juice	ju**ice** on **ice** is best
juncture	jun**ct**ure in **CT** (Connecticut)
junior	**uni**cycle is a j**uni**or bicycle
jurisdiction	juris**diction** spoke with excellent **diction**
justify	**I** will just**i**fy it
justice	**justice** will be served if you give me **just ice**
juvenile	e**ven**tually, we all stop being ju**ven**iles
kangaroo	b**ang** the k**ang**aroo exhibit
kayak	**Kay**, from **AK** is in front and back of **kayak**
kennel	**Ken** takes his dog **Nel** to **kennel**
kept	ke**pt** the **p**urple **t**ea in the cabinet
kerosene	poured ke**rose**ne on the **rose**
kettle	**2 T** bags in the ke**tt**le
khaki	**ha**! You look funny in those k**ha**kis
kidney	**y** do we have a kidne**y**
kilowatt	**kilo** in a **kilo**watt
kindergarten	**ten kind** kids are in **kind**ergar**ten**
kindle	**kind**le of wood is **kind**
kingdom	hey **King**, **do** I belong in the **Kingdo**m
kitchen	**hen** is in the kitc**hen**
knotted	who's k**notted**? **Not Ted**

knowledge	**know** what's on the **ledge** and get **knowledge**
label	**Abe** will apply the l**abe**l
labor	**lab or** any other place, there's always **labor**
laboratory	a **rat** between the **O**'s is in lab**orato**ry
lacerate	Dr. had to **lace** up **lace**ration
ladle	**able ladle** will do the job
laminate	take a **min**ute to la**min**ate
landlord	**Lord** over **land** is **landlord**
landscape	**land's cap** is over **landscap**e
language	can you **gauge** any lan**guage**
languish	**langui**sh on any **langu**age
lantern	put the lant**ern** in the **ER**
lapel	**ape** wears a pin on his l**ape**l
larceny	stealing a **cent** is lar**cen**y
larynx	**y** is e**N**velope being **X**-rayed on my lar**ynx**
lascivious	**IOU** an apology for my lasciv**iou**s remark
lasso	la**sso** **2 s**'s
lately	**latel**y I've been **late**
latitude	get **at it** and check its l**atit**ude
laughable	if you're **able** to **laugh** you're **laughable**
laughter	there's laught**er** in the **ER**
launch	astronauts eat **a**pples for **lunch** before **launch**
laundry	**a u**! **Dry** the l**aundry**
lavaliere	**lavalie**re microphone destroyed by **lava**, no **lie**
lavatory	**lava** flowed into the **lava**tory
lavender	the f**ender** was lav**ender**
lawyer	"**yer**" **lawyer** knows the **law**
laxative	la**x**ative is by the **ax**
laziness	**I**, for one, have never been known for laz**i**ness
league	**u** **e**valuate every leag**ue**
leakage	**age** of pipe caused leak**age**
lecture	take a pi**cture** during le**cture**
ledger	**ledger** is on the **ledge**

legalize	it's time to lega**lize** **Liz**
legend	**leg** at the **end** is a **legend**
legible	**leg** that writes is not **leg**ible
legislature	**leg is** in **legis**lature
legitimate	**leg** of **mate** is **legi**ti**mate**
leisure	**I sure** hope this is a lei**sure** trip
lemonade	place an **Ad** for a lemon**ade** stand
length	**g**, why is a G in len**G**th
lenient	**Len** and **I** were **lenient** when we **ent**ered
leprechaun	my a**unt** is a leprech**aun**
lethal	it's **lethal** to **let Hal** hold gun
lethargy	**let Har**ry be **lethar**gy
lettuce	do **u** like lett**u**ce
liability	there's **ability** in li**ability**
liaison	the r**aison** is a li**aison**
liberal	the **ERA** is lib**era**l
library	learn about **Bra**zil in the li**bra**ry
license	he has a **lic**ense to kill **lice**
licorice	**Co** (company) puts **rice** in its li**corice**
lieutenant	if you **lie u ten ant**s, I'll call the **lieutenant**
ligament	tore a li**game**nt in the **game**
likable	**no E** is **likable**
likely	**Ike** is l**ike**ly to win
lilac	**c** the lila**c**
limousine	**mous**e is in the li**mous**ine
Lincoln	Linco**l**n lived in a **l**og cabin
lingerie	don't **linger** near the **linger**ie
linoleum	**ole** lin**ole**um
liquid	to drink that liqu**id** you need to show **ID**
literacy	**ERA** believes in lit**era**cy
literature	**ERA** puts out lit**era**ture
livelihood	**I** have a livel**i**hood
loathe	take an **oath** to l**oath**e

locomotive	lo**co**m**o**tive is **o**pen
loneliness	lone**line**ss of the **line**
longevity	long**ev**ity of **ev**ening
lotion	m**otion** for l**otion**
lottery	lott**er**y in the **ER**
lounge	**un**wind in the lo**un**ge
lubricant	**Ant** is lubric**ant**
luggage	3 **G**'s are in my lu**gg**age
luminescent	**mine** is lu**mine**scent
luncheonette	**che**w in lun**che**onette
luscious	**IOU** a lusc**iou**s dessert
luxury	l**ux**ury for your **X** to be between **U**
lying	**ying** is l**ying**
lymph	**y me** with the sore l**ym**ph
macaroni	ma**car**oni in **car**
machete	**Ma**, **Chet** has **machet**e
machinery	machin**er**y is in the **ER**
magazine	catch some **z's** while reading maga**z**ine
magic	**i c** mag**ic**
magistrate	mag**is**trate **is** right
magnet	mag**net**ic **net**
magnificence	mag**nificence** of this word; **2 I**'s and **2 E**'s
magnitude	mag**ni**tude is **i**ncredible
mahogany	**ma hogs any mahogany** desk
maintenance	**Nan** was in mainte**nan**ce
majority	**Major** is in **major**ity
making	**Ma**, the **King** is **making** a mess
malice	**Ma**, **lice** are a **malice**
malicious	**i c IOU** a mal**icious** remark
malign	Muhammad **Ali** throws a m**ali**gn punch
mammal	3 **mammal**s (3 M's) are all named **Al**
manageable	**man** with **age** is **manage**able
mandatory	**a Tory** was mand**atory**

109

maneuver	**Mane u** brush must be **maneu**vered
manger	**anger** in m**anger**
manicure	**I c u r** getting a man**icur**e
manifesto	**I** wrote a man<u>i</u>festo
mantelpiece	put the **tel**ephone on man**tel**piece
manufacture	what are the **fact**s about this manu**fact**ure
manuscript	hey **man**, **u script** the **manuscript**
margarine	**g**, I like mar**g**arine
maritime	**r**ight **time** to ma**ritime**
market	**e**verything is at the mark**et**
marmalade	**Ma**, **Ma**, can I have some **marma**lade
marriage	**I** do in marr<u>i</u>age
martyr	**y** be a mart**y**r
marvelous	I **marvel** at **marvel**ous paintings
masculine	**c u line** up by the mas**culine** man
Massachusetts	**a chu** (sneeze) at **Mass** and you **set** things off
massacre	Boston **Massacre** in **Mass** covered small **acre**
massage	**massage** during **Mass** took **age**s off me
masquerade	**Qu**een is at the mas**qu**erade party
material	**mate** in **RI** named **Al**, has **material**
maternity	in**tern** works in ma**tern**ity ward
mathematics	**hem** your dress in math**em**atics class
mattress	relieve s**tress** by sleeping on mat**tress**
matriarch	**mat** in **RI** under **arch** is for **matriarch**
matrimony	**mat** on a **rim** is in **matrim**ony
mature	**u** are mat**u**re
maverick	**Rick** is a mave**rick**
maximum	**Max** and **I** are **mum** to the **maximum**
mayonnaise	put **on** pr**aise** with may**onnaise**
meadow	heard a **meow** in the **meadow** so I placed an **Ad**
mechanic	**cha** ching, me**cha**nic charged me more money
medal	**Al** won a med**al**
medallion	**med** student **Al** saved **lion**; received **medallion**

meddle	**2 d**'s are me**dd**ling
medicine	**medic** uses **medicin**e **in** patients
mediocre	**IOC** (Int'l Olympic Comm.) is med**ioc**re
Mediterranean	**R**eagan **r**an **e**arly **at n**oon by Medite**rrean**
medium	**I, um**, will have a med**ium** chocolate shake
melancholy	**cho**ke melan**cho**ly man
memorial	**memo** in **RI** is for **Al** about the **memorial**
menace	**men** who think they are an **ace** are a **menace**
merchandise	merchand**ise** will r**ise**
mesmerize	catch **z's** while you're mesmeri**z**ed
messenger	**en**ter mess**en**ger
metallic	met**all**ic medal is **tall**
metamorphosis	**o sis** is metamorph**osis**
metaphor	**tap** the me**tap**hor
meticulous	**I c u** being very met**icu**lous
metropolitan	**polit**e people live in metro**polit**an areas
mileage	**mile** and **age** are in **mileage**
military	mili**tar**y man is in **tar**
millennium	**Len** celebrated new mil**len**nium
millionaire	**lion** leaped into **air** when becoming mil**lionair**e
miniature	I walked the mini**at**ure **A**ppalachian **T**rail
minimum	**Mum**, with **mini**skirt, gave me the **minimum**
miracle	m**ira**cle when you invest in an **IRA**
mirror	mirr**or** is shaped like an **O**
miscellaneous	miscel**lane**ous **cell** phone **an**d **e**ar piece
mischievous	**Chie**f was mis**chie**vous
miserable	**is** the **ERA** m**isera**ble
misspell	a **miss miss**pelled
moisture	j**oist** has m**oist**ure
monarch	on **Mon**day **monarch** is at the **arch**
morgue	**g, u** like the mor**gu**e, don't you
morsel	give the mors**el** to the **el**ephant
mortgage	mor**t**gage is calculated to a **T**

mosquito	don't **quit** or mos**quit**o will bite you
mustache	**ache** to grow a must**ache**
mustard	don't be **tard**y passing mus**tard**
mysterious	**IOU** a myster**iou**s look
nastiness	**tin** was full of nas**tin**ess
national	**Nation** is in **national**
nausea	nau**sea** starts in the **sea**
navigable	**I gab** when ship is nav**igab**le
nebulous	**lous**y to be nebu**lous**
necessary	the **cess**pools **are** ne**cessar**y
necessity	ne**cess**ity for a **cess**pool
neglect	don't negle**ct CT** (Connecticut)
negligence	neglig**ence** in Provid**ence**
negotiate	**I ate** after I negot**iate**d
neighbor	hell**o** neighb**or**
neither	**it** is in ne**it**her
nervous	**ER** makes me n**er**vous
neurotic	**u rot** when you're ne**urot**ic
neutral	**UT** (Utah) is ne**ut**ral
neutralize	**u** must ne**ut**ralize it
nicely	**nice**ly is **nice**
nickel	**el**ephant ate my nick**el**
nicotine	ni**cot**ine is in the **cot**
niece	gave my n**iece** p**ie**
nocturnal	bats are no**cturn**al and **c** every **turn**
nominate	he **ate in** so nom**inate** him
nonchalant	**Hal** and **ant** are nonc**halant**
normal	**Norm** and **Al** are **normal**
nostalgic	Mr. **Al G.**, **I c** you are nost**algic**
notable	**no table** is **notable**
noticeable	**able** to **notice** you're **noticeable**
notorious	notor**ious IOU**
nourish	**our** food will n**our**ish us

nuclear	be **clear** with nu**clear**
nudity	covering **IT** isn't nud**it**y
nuisance	dog **is** a nu**is**ance
nullification	null**ification** of **3 I**'s
numb	thum**b** is num**b**
numerous	to **me**, this is how nu**me**rous is spelled
nursery	**nurse** was at **nurse**ry
oath	take an o**ath** to take a b**ath**
obedience	rather **die** than to go to obe**die**nce school
obese	**bes**t were o**bes**e
obey	b**e** a good boy and o**be**y
obituary	if it **bit u** you'll be in o**bitu**ary pages
object	obje**ct** to living in **CT** (Connecticut)
oblique	**liqu**id is ob**lique**
obnoxious	**ox**, who didn't pay his **IOU**, is obn**oxiou**s
obscene	the **scene** was ob**scene**
observance	**van** was under obser**van**ce
obsession	ob**session** was in **session**
obsolete	**sole** of my shoe is ob**sole**te
obstinate	**tin** I **ate** was ob**tinate**
obvious	obv**iou**sly an **IOU** needs to be drawn up
occasion	o**cca**sionally she pays by **CC** when low on **$**
occupancy	hotel o**ccupan**cy accepts **CC** in a **pan**
occupant	I **c cup** and **ant** as the o**ccupant**s
occur	did it o**cc**ur to you to use your **CC** (credit card)
octopus	**top** of oc**topus** were two of **us**
odyssey	**y** is od**y**ssey spelled with a **Y**
official	keep **off**, **I c I** should call **offici**al
often	I of**ten** say of**ten ten** times
omelet	**let me** eat o**melet**
ominous	**In** om**in**ous building
omission	**mission** in o**mission**
opera	**ERA** is at op**era**

113

operate	**ERA** knows how to op**era**te
opinion	who's **opinion** was it to put **p**eas in **onion**
opponent	**2 P**'s are o**ppon**ents. It's tied at **one**
opportunity	great op**portunit**y to meet at **port** with **unit**
oppose	I'm op**pose**d to **pose**
optimism	**Tim** has op**tim**ism
orator	**o**rator **o**pens his mouth
orchestra	instruments of or**chest**ra are in **chest**
orchid	**c** where he **hid** or**chid**
ordinary	letter **A** is ordin**a**ry
organization	**organ** belongs to **organ**ization
origin	what's the ori**gin** of **gin**
ornament	let's **name** the or**name**nt
ostrich	**Rich** owns an ost**rich**
outrageous	so much **rage** was out**rage**ous
overwhelm	overw**helm**ing to see him at **helm**
oxygen	get to **X** and **Y** and you're out of o**xy**gen
oyster	b**oys** ate **oys**ter
pageant	**page** with **an**t was at **pageant**
panorama	pan**o**rama view is like this: **O**
paradise	this **is** parad**is**e
parallel	bowling **alley** is par**alle**l to the snack bar
paralyze	last 2 letters of alphabet, **Y** & **Z**, are paral**yz**ed
patient	**Pa**, **tie patie**nt down
particular	**I c u** are very part**icu**lar
patriot	**Pat**, a **patriot**, caused **riot**
pavilion	there's a **lion** in the pavi**lion**
pedestrian	**Ed** hit the pe**d**estrian
penitentiary	**2 I**'s at each end of **tent are** in pen**itentia**ry
Pennsylvania	**Sylvia** is from Penn**sylv**ania
perimeter	**rim** is at pe**rim**eter
persevere	per**severe** when it's **severe**
persistence	succeeding after **ten** shows your persis**ten**ce

personnel	**person** named **Nel** works in **personnel**
perspiration	**e**very **i**ndividual has pe**rspi**ration
pessimist	he's a pessi**mist** about **mist**
petroleum	the **role** of pet**role**um
phenomenon	**hen**'s **omen** was a p**henomen**on
Philadelphia	**Phil** ran an **Ad** in **Philade**lphia
philanthropy	**Phil** and the **ant** are into **philant**hropy
philharmonic	**Phil**'s **harm**ing the **philharm**onic orchestra
physical	**i c Al** needs a phys**ical**
physician	phy**sic**ian helps those who are **sic**k
physique	**que**en has a nice physi**que**
pigeon	**pig** **e**ats **on** the **pigeon**
pioneer	**one** pi**one**er
plausible	**sib**ling is plau**sib**le
plumber	p**lumber** works in **lumber**
poignant	**gnat** is poi**gnant**
pollute	according to **poll**, it's not nice to **poll**ute
popular	**Lar**ry is pop**ular**
possession	**4** **S**'s are in po**ssess**ion
poultry	**try** poul**try**
precedent	if you **cede** you'll set a pre**ced**ent
precinct	pre**cinct** moved from **Cin**cinnati to **CT**
preference	p**refer**en**ce** is to use all **E**'s
prejudice	don't show preju**dice** before you toss **dice**
preliminary	letter **A** is in the prelimin**a**ry
premonition	**Mo** has a pre**mo**nition
preposterous	**poster** is pre**poster**ous
prevalent	**vale** was pre**val**ent
privilege	it's a privi**lege** to have a **leg**
pronunciation	**Nun** has great pro**nun**ciation
proprietor	pry **o**pen proprie**to**r's door
propulsion	pro**puls**ion causes my **puls**e to rise
prospectus	**US** (United States) companies have a prospect**us**

proximity	what's the pro**x**imity to **X**
Puerto Rico	**p u**! send the **ER** team **to** **Puerto** Rico
puncture	pun**c**ture the **C**
qualify	did **Al** qu**al**ify
quantity	**it** has a large quant**ity**
quarantine	**ran** to get **tin** from the qua**rantin**e
quarrel	b**arrel** had a qu**arrel**
quarter	there's a **quart**er in the **quart** of milk
questionnaire	2 **n**'s needed **air** to fill out questio**nnair**e
quick	qu**ick**, I'm s**ick**
quizzes	catch some **z**'s when taking qui**zz**es
quizzical	**2 z**'s between my **I**'s are qui**zzi**cal
raccoon	ra**cc**oon paid by **CC** (credit card)
radiant	Princess **Di** was ra**di**ant
radical	**I**, **Cal**, am rad**ical**
raffle	r**affle** for w**affle**
rainy	rai**ny** in **NY**
raisin	**sin** not to like rai**sin**s
rampage	**ram**, who tore **page**, was on a **rampage**
raspberry	who put the **p**ea in the ras**p**berry dish
ratio	**rat** is part of **rat**io
rationalize	**Liz** had to rationa**liz**e
rattle	b**attle** for r**attle**
razor	don't **o**pen your mouth when using a raz**o**r
realize	**Liz** did rea**liz**e
rebellion	**lion** showed rebel**lion**
rebuttal	every **butt** has a re**butt**al
receipt	**E**very **i**ndividual **p**aying **t**olls; get a rec**eipt**
recognize	did you re**cog**nize the **cog** rail
recommend	we re**commen**d a dot **com** for **men**
recovery	after being in **ER** you go to recov**er**y room
recruit	rec**ruit** f**ruit**
recurrence	**en**d recurr**en**ce

116

reference	I got an **e**xcellent r**eferenc**e from all the **E's**
refrigerator	**o**pen refrigerat**o**r
refugee	**gee**, are you a refu**gee**
rehabilitate	**I** have to rehabil**i**tate
reindeer	**in** come **deer**, including re**indeer**
religious	relig**ious IOU**
relinquish	relin**q**uish the **Q** stick
reminisce	we had a **mini** re**minisc**e in **SC** (South Carolina)
remittance	remit**tan**ce form is **tan**
renaissance	**is San**dy at the rena**issan**ce
rendezvous	**z z** to rend**ez**vous
repel	re**pel** from the **pel**ting of rain
repertory	**ER** has a rep**er**tory
reprieve	**I** repr**ieve** in the **eve**
reprimand	by getting on **rim And**y was rep**rimand**ed
resemblance	there was a **bland** resem**blan**ce
reservation	**Erv** has a res**erv**ation
residence	my res**idence** is in Prov**idence**
residual	**dual** for resi**dual**
resign	re**sign** to put up **sign**
resilience	**I lie** when I say he has res**ilie**nce
resistance	**sis** has re**sistan**ce for **tan** outfits
responsible	**I** am respons**i**ble
restaurant	**taur**us ate at res**taur**ant
resumption	**ump** has res**ump**tion
retaliate	**I ate** to retal**iate**
reversible	**sib**ling has a rever**sib**le jacket
rhetoric	**he** is full of r**h**etoric
rhinoceros	**c** the rhino**c**eros
rhododendron	**do den**s at **Ron**'s have rho**dodendron**
rhubarb	eat r**hub**arb in **hub**
rhyme	r**hym**e is in **hym**n book
rhythm	**h**ungry **y**ouths have r**hy**thm

ridiculous	**I c u** are rid**icu**lous
righteous	"A" is only the vowel not present in r**ight****eou**s
rotary	wet **tar** around ro**tar**y
roulette	**o u let** him win at r**oulet**te
routine	going **out** then **in** is a r**outin**e
sacred	**red sac** is **sacred**
sacrifice	**I** sacr**i**fice
salami	**Sal**, **am I** the only one who likes **salami**
salmon	**Sal** caught a **salmon** on **Mon**day
sapphire	**sap** who **hire**d **sapp****hire** salesman was fired
satellite	I can **tell** if it's a sat**ell**ite
satisfactory	**factory** is satis**factory**
sausage	**USA** loves its sa**usa**ge
scenery	**scene** in **scene**ry
schedule	**che**ck the s**che**dule
scheme	**sch**eme at **sch**ool
science	when frogs d**ie** it's sc**ie**nce
scissors	s**ci****ssors** cut **s**'s into 4 parts
secretary	**secretar**y with a **secret** does **A**+ work
seize	**se**ize the **SE** (SouthEast)
sergeant	**Sergeant** had to **serge** toward **ant**
shepherd	**Ph**d was a she**ph**erd
shrubbery	**rubber** is in sh**rubber**y
siege	during s**ie**ge soldiers would d**ie**
signature	**nature** has a wonderful sig**nature**
significant	**ant** is signific**ant**
silence	**Len** said si**len**ce was in order
silhouette	**hou**se is in sil**hou**ette
similar	**Lar** is simi**lar** to **Lar**ry
sincerely	e**arly** letters end with e**ly**, sincer**ely** yours
society	fashion, money, **ie**…soc**ie**ty
solemn	**sole** from **MN** (Minnesota) gave **solemn** oath
sophisticate	**his cat** is sop**hist****icat**ed

118

sophomore	so**phomore**s stay on **pho**ne **more**
sovereign	King **reign**s in a sove**reign** nation
spaghetti	**spa** near **ghett**o serves **spaghett**i
special	any **spec** is **spec**ial
statistic	**at** and **is** make up a st**atis**tic
stomach	**hold E**, I have a stom**ach ach**e
strength	**eng**ine has str**eng**th
subscription	**script** in sub**script**ion
suburb	**u** live in sub**u**rb
suede	**Sue** is dressed in **sue**de
sufficient	**I c I** am suff**ici**ent
sugar	**UGA** (Univ. of GA) grows s**ugar**
summary	**Mary** has the sum**mary**
superintendent	**superintendent** is **super in ten dents**
surgery	patient was **surge**d into **surger**y
surveillance	**veil Lance** wore was shown on sur**veillance**
sword	**word** in s**word**
syllable	**2 L**'s in sy**llable** were **able** to stand back to back
sympathy	have sym**path**y as I walk down **path**
symphony	there's a **phony** in sym**phony**
symptom	**p**ea **Tom** ate is giving him a sym**ptom**
syndicate	**dicate** a letter to syn**dicate**
syrup	**y** use s**y**rup
system	**stem** in sy**stem**
tactics	his **tact**ics are not a good **tact**
tailor	tail**o**r threads needle through **O**
Taiwan	**ai**n't it nice to be in T**ai**wan
taking	**King** is ta**king** everything
tangible	a **GI** is tan**gi**ble
tariff	**if tar** is put down there is a **tarif**f
tattoo	Mr. **Tat** wants a **tattoo, too**
temperature	he has a **temper** when **temper**ature rises
temporarily	**tempo** is **tempo**rarily changed

tenacious	**c, IOU** for being tena**ciou**s
tendon	**Don** has **ten tendon**s
Tennessee	2 **S**'s and **E**'s going to Tenne**ssee**
terminal	**in** term**in**al
terrain	**rain** on ter**rain**
terrible	**rib**s are ter**rib**le
terrific	**if I c** you it will be terr**ific**
territory	**RI** (Rhode Island) makes up a small ter**ri**tory
testament	tes**tame**nt is **tame**
testify	**if** I pass **test** I'll will **testif**y
texture	**text**book has a nice **text**ure
Thailand	**hail** a cab in T**hail**and
theme	**theme** is **the** and **me**
therapeutic	**ape** is ther**ape**utic
thermostat	**o**pen therm**o**stat
thesaurus	**the taurus** is in a **the**s**aurus**
thorough	it's **rough** to be tho**rough**
thousand	thou**sand** grains of **sand**
threshold	**hold** her through thres**hold**
thumb	th**umb** is n**umb**
tobacco	use a **CC** (credit card) to buy toba**cco**
tolerant	**ERA** is tol**era**nt
tomato	to**mat**o is on **mat**
tomorrow	**Tom** will have s**orrow tomorrow**
tongue	**on** her t**on**gue
torpedo	**Ed** fires torp**ed**o
tragedy	if you **rag** on **Ed** it's a t**raged**y
treasurer	are you **sure** you're the trea**sure**r
triumph	**ump** will always tri**ump**h
twelfth	the tw**elf**th **elf** is here
tying	**Ty** is t**y**ing bundles
ukulele	play uk**ule**le during y**ule**tide
ultimatum	**Tim** has an ul**tim**atum

unanimous	**I'm** unan**im**ous
uniform	there's a **form** in the uni**form**
unique	**Que**en is uni**que**
unison	**son** and **I** are in un**ison**
universe	**universe** has a **uni verse**
university	**varsity** attends uni**versity**
usually	**all** are usu**all**y here
vaccination	pay va**cc**ination on a **CC** (credit card)
vacuum	**u, u** must vac**uu**m
valentine	drank **ale** on V**ale**ntine's Day
valuable	**u** are **able**, therefore, you're val**uable**
vanilla	I say **nill** to va**nill**a
variable	vari**able** is **able**
variety	before you d**ie** try var**ie**ty
various	in **Rio** two of **us** did va**rious** things
vegetable	vege**table** is on **table**
vehement	I ve**hem**ently request you lower your **hem**
vehicle	say **hi** from ve**hi**cle
ventriloquist	ventril**o**quist never **o**pens his mouth
verbal	**Al** is verb**al**
verification	**if I c** you need ver**ific**ation I'll tell you
versatile	**tile** is versa**tile**
versus	it's them vers**us us**
vertical	**I c Al** is vert**ical**
veterinary	**Erin** goes to vet**erin**ary school
vicinity	**Cin**cinnati is in vi**cin**ity
victim	**c Tim**, he's a vi**ctim**
village	what is the **age** of the vill**age**
vinegar	**vine**gar is on **vine**
violence	vio**len**ce followed **Len**
violin	play viol**in in**doors
virtue	bl**ue** virt**ue**
vitamin	**am I** supposed to take a vit**ami**n

vocabulary	starting with **A** know your vocabul**a**ry
voice	**ice** is in your vo**ice**
volume	**u** and **me** create a loud vol**ume**
volunteer	volunt**eer** to shoot a d**eer**
wagon	**on** the wag**on**
waken	**Ken** had to wa**ken**
wallet	**Al, let** him borrow your w**allet**
walnut	**Al** ate a wa**l**nut
warden	**warden** is at **war** in **den**
warehouse	**are** we at the w**are**house
warrior	**warrio**r in **war** creates a **rio**t
wary	M**ary** is w**ary**
weapon	l**eap** with a w**eap**on
weather	H**eather** enjoys the w**eather**
wedding	**Ed**, you **ding** dong, don't be late for w**edding**
Wednesday	they **wed** on **Wed**nesday
weird	**we** are **we**ird
western	west**er**n was shown in **ER**
whether	**wh**ether it's **wh**ite or black we'll never know
whisk	say **hi** when being w**hi**sked away
whistle	whis**t**le blown for **t**imeout
Wisconsin	**con** commits a **sin** so send him to Wis**consin**
wither	**It** wi**t**hers away
wizard	L**iz** is a w**iz**ard
wolves	**LV** (Las Vegas) has many wo**lv**es
womb	**w**ow, **o**ne **m**ore **b**aby is in **womb**
wondrous	**o u** are wondr**ou**s
world	w**o**rld is shaped like an **O**
worship	**or** you can w**orship** in **ship**
worth	**or** just tell me what it's w**or**th
wound	w**ound** is r**ound**
wrestle	**rest** when you w**rest**le
writing	**I ting**le when wr**iting**

122

Xavier	**vie** for position at Xa**vie**r
xylophone	aim for **X**, don't ask **Y**, and play **xy**lophone
yacht	**ach**e to be on a y**ach**t
yesterday	yest**er**day I was in the **ER**
yogurt	won't get h**urt** if you eat yog**urt**
youngster	young**st**er stood on **ST** (street)
zeal	z**eal** for a m**eal**
zenith	**it** is in zen**it**h
zephyr	**hy**drate when a zep**hy**r approaches
zinc	z**inc**, **inc**.
zoology	bring **log** to zoo**log**y department

Summary

The common thread throughout the book is attaching new information to what you already know. We did it on every page.

When studying, look for clues helping you retain the information by asking yourself, *what do I already know*? Then, connect what you know to what you want to know. You'll be able to do this in any subject.

Listen in the classroom, take notes, ask questions, do your homework nightly, and always be ready to learn.

ADVANCED SECTION

Remembering the Periodic Table

1 H																	2 He
3 Li	4 Be											5 B	6 C	7 N	8 O	9 F	10 Ne
11 Na	12 Mg											13 Al	14 Si	15 P	16 S	17 Cl	18 Ar
19 K	20 Ca	21 Sc	22 Ti	23 V	24 Cr	25 Mn	26 Fe	27 Co	28 Ni	29 Cu	30 Zn	31 Ga	32 Ge	33 As	34 Se	35 Br	36 Kr
37 Rb	38 Sr	39 Y	40 Zr	41 Nb	42 Mo	43 Tc	44 Ru	45 Rh	46 Pd	47 Ag	48 Cd	49 In	50 Sn	51 Sb	52 Te	53 I	54 Xe
55 Cs	56 Ba		72 Hf	73 Ta	74 W	75 Re	76 Os	77 Ir	78 Pt	79 Au	80 Hg	81 Tl	82 Pb	83 Bi	84 Po	85 At	86 Rn
87 Fr	88 Ra		104 Rf	105 Db	106 Sg	107 Bh	108 Hs	109 Mt	110 Ds	111 Rg	112 Cn	113 Uut	114 Fl	115 Uup	116 Lv	117 Uus	118 Uuo

57 La	58 Ce	59 Pr	60 Nd	61 Pm	62 Sm	63 Eu	64 Gd	65 Tb	66 Dy	67 Ho	68 Er	69 Tm	70 Yb	71 Lu
89 Ac	90 Th	91 Pa	92 U	93 Np	94 Pu	95 Am	96 Cm	97 Bk	98 Cf	99 Es	100 Fm	101 Md	102 No	103 Lr

A s you can see from the chart, the Periodic Table is composed of codes and numbers. Before we begin to learn these, we must create a system for connecting each symbol and number into a memorable connection.

In the English language there are ten (10) consonant sounds. There are also ten (10) digits represented from 0-9. Each digit is coded to a consonant letter. Keep in mind, the vowels, *a, e, i, o, u*, as well as *w, h*, and *y* have no value. We begin with the digit 0.

0 = s, soft c, z   Words such as *z*ebra, *c*elery, and *s*oft create a sissing sound. As a reminder, Zero ends with <u>0</u>

1 = t or d   *T* and *d* make similar sounds, as in *d*esk and *t*est. As a reminder, the typewritten *t* and *d* have <u>one</u> downstroke

2 = n   typewritten *n* has <u>two</u> downstrokes

3 = m   typewritten *m* has <u>three</u> downstrokes

4 = r   fou<u>R</u> ends with *R*

5 = L   roman numeral <u>50</u> is <u>L</u>

6 = sh, ch, j, soft g. Note how these sounds are similar, as in *j*udge, *sh*oe, *ch*urch, *g*inger, and *j*oy, As a reminder, mirror image of a *6* resembles a *j*.

7 = k, q, hard c and g. Look closely and you'll see an upside *7* in *K*. Words such as, *c*ard, *g*irl, *q*uick, and *k*ettle begin with the *k* sound.

8 = f, v, ph, gh cursive *f* resembles an *8*. Note how the words, *f*reedom, *v*ote, *ph*oto, and cou*gh* have the same sound.

9 = p and b mirror image of *9* resembles *P*. Words such as, *b*oy and *p*lay have a popping sound.

Below are 118 numbers with corresponding words. Each number represents the atomic number of the Periodic Table.

1. hiDe	33. MaMa	65. SHeLL	97. BiKe
2. hoNey	34. haMMeR	66. CHoo CHoo	98. BehaVe
3. haM	35. MiLe	67. SHaKe	99. BaBy
4. haiR	36. MaTCH	68. SHaVe	100. DaiSeS
5. iLL	37. MuG	69. SHiP	101. TeST
6. SHoe	38. MoVe	70. KiSS	102. Day'S INN
7. Guy	39. MaP	71. KiTe	103. DaZe Me
8. heaVy	40. hoRSe	72. waGoN	104. TaSeR
9. hoP	41. RoT	73. GaMe	105. TaSSeL
10. diZZy	42. RuN	74. CaR	106. DoSaGe
11. DaD	43. RooM	75. eaGLe	107. DeSK
12. ToN	44. RoaR	76. CouCH	108. DeCeiVe
13. DuMb	45. ReaLLy	77. CaKe	109. Day SPa
14. waTeR	46. RiCH	78. CouGH	110. ToaDS
15. DoLL	47. RuG	79. KeeP	111. DaTeD
16. TouCH	48. RouGH	80. oFFiCe	112. TiTaN
17. DeCK	49. RoPe	81. FooD	113. TaTuM
18. TV	50. wheeLS	82. PHoNe	114. DeTouR
19. TuB	51. LaDy	83. FoaM	115. DeTaiL
20. NoiSy	52. aLoNe	84. FiRe	116. hoT DiSH
21. wiNDow	53. LaMb	85. FLy	117. hoT DoG
22. oNioN	54. LawyeR	86. FiSH	118. weT DoVe
23. gNoMe	55. LiLy	87. VaC	
24. NaRRow	56. LeaSH	88. FiFe	
25. NaiL	57. LoG	89. FBI	
26. eNJoy	58. LaVa	90. BuS	
27. NeCK	59. heLP	91. BoaT	
28. NaVy	60. CHeeSe	92. PoNy	
29. NaP	61. SHuT	93. BoMb	
30. MiCe	62. CHaiN	94. PooR	
31. MaD	63. JiMMy	95. BLue	
32. MaNy	64. CHeeR	96. BuSH	

Note: numbers from 10-19 have either a bold **D** or **T** and are capitalized.

Numbers 20-29 begin with the letter *n*. The second **bold letter** represents the other number. For instance, *29* codes to an *N* and a *P*, as in **NaP**.

Some words begin with vowels as in *onion* (22), or the letter *w*, as in *window*. (21). However, those letters have no value since we're only interested in consonant sounds.

Double letters together are coded to only one number, as in the *m* in ha**MM**e**R** (34) or the *n* in **Day'S i<u>NN</u>**.

The word **mat<u>ch</u>** codes to 36, not 316, because it's a quick *ch* sound. The *t* is not pronounced.

Remember, it's only the sound that keys into the number.

Spend time learning the system. These words will be linked to each element.

Pathways for Remembering the Periodic Table

Examples...

11=Sodium (Na)= <u>N</u>ever <u>a</u>ttempt pouring <u>soda</u> (Sodium) on <u>Dad</u>

<u>Beginning letters</u> of the <u>first two words</u> in the sentence <u>represent the symbol</u> for that element. In the example above it's ... *never attempt* for <u>*Na*</u> (Sodium).

Within each sentence is a recognizable word aiding us to remember the element. In the example above, it's *soda*, which sounds similar to *sodium*. Immediately following this clue is the (element name in parenthesis)

<u>Last word </u> in the sentence, which is <u>underlined</u>, <u>represents the atomic number</u> taken from the <u>phonetic alphabet</u> (see page 23). In the example above, it's *Dad*; representing number 11.

If the word is repeated, (without parenthesis) the element has only a <u>one letter symbol</u>. See example below.

6 = Carbon (C) = <u>Cars</u>, yes <u>cars</u> (Carbon), ran over my <u>shoe</u>

Since cars is repeated, the element has one letter for its symbol. Note the last word is *shoe*, which represents 6 in the phonetic alphabet.

This will be the pattern for the 118 elements.

Note that many of the elements end with the letters *ium*.

Below are 118 numbers with corresponding words. Each number represents the atomic number of the Periodic Table.

1= Hydrogen (H) = **Hide**, yes **hide** behind his <u>hide</u>
Hide sounds like *Hydrogen*. The word *hide* is repeated, so it must be one symbol (H). The last word is *hide*; coded to the number 1.

2=Helium (He)= **Heel** (Helium) **e**ntering helium balloon is made of <u>honey</u>
Heel sounds like *Helium*. The first word begins with *H* (Heel); the next word begins with *e* (entering). Therefore, the symbol must be *He*. The last word is *honey*; coded to the number 2.

3= Lithium (Li) = **Lit** **i**nto (Lithium) <u>ham</u>
Lit sounds like *Lithium*. The first word begins with *L* (Lit); the next word begins with *i* (into). Therefore, the symbol must be (Li). The last word is *ham*; coded to the number 3.

4=Berylium (Be)= **Berry's** (Berylium) **e**scaped from her <u>hair</u>

5=Boron (B)= **Bore**, **yes bore**, Ron (Boron) and he'll be <u>ill</u>

6=Carbon (C)= **Cars**, **yes cars** (Carbon), ran over my <u>shoe</u>

7=Nitrogen (N) = **Night**, yes **night**, (Nitrogen), <u>guy</u>

8=Oxygen (O) = **Ox**, yes <u>**ox**</u> (Oxygen), is <u>heavy</u>

9=Fluorine (F) = **Flu** season, yes **flu** season, (Fluorine) makes me <u>hop</u>

10=Neon (Ne) = **Neon** (Neon) **e**arly lights make me <u>dizzy</u>

11=Sodium (Na)= **N**ever **a**ttempt pouring **soda** (Sodium) on <u>Dad</u>

12=Magnesium (Mg)=**Magazine** (Magnesium) **g**iven to me weighs a <u>ton</u>

13=Aluminum (Al) = **Aluminum** (Aluminum) **l**adders are <u>dumb</u>

14=Silicon=(Si) = **Silly** (Silicon) **i**ce contains <u>water</u>

15=Phosphorous (P) = **Photo**, yes **Photo** (Phosphorous) graph my <u>doll</u>

16=Sulfur (S)= **Sell fur**, yes **Sell fur**, (Sulfur) but don't <u>touch</u>

130

17=Chlrorine (Cl)= **Chlorine** (Chlorine) lays across deck

18=Argon (Ar) = **Are gowns** (Argon) radiant on TV

19=Potassium (K) = **Kind**, yes **kind**, pot (Potassium) belly pigs in tub

20=Calcium (Ca)=**Calculations** (Calcium) always makes me noisy

21=Scandium (Sc) **Scan** (Scandium) color pictures onto window

22=Titanium (Ti) **Tie** into the tan (Titanium) onion

23=Vandadium (V) **Van**, yes **van** (Vandadium), drove over a gnome

24=Chromium (Cr) **Chrome** (Chromium) railing is narrow

25=Manganese (Mn) **Man**, named Ganese (Manganese), sat on a nail

26=Iron (Fe)= **Few** elephants can **iron** (Iron); not something they enjoy

27=Cobalt (Co)= **Colored orange bolts** (Cobalt) hang from my neck

28=Nickel (Ni)=**Nickels** (Nickel) inside the Navy

29=Copper (Cu)= **Copper** (Copper) unicorns nap

30= Zinc (Zn) = **Zinc** (Zinc) never messes with mice

31= Gallium (Ga) = **Gals** (Gallium) always are mad

32 = Germanium (Ge) = **Germs** (Germanium) enter many

33= Arsenic (As) = **Arsonists** (Arsenic) start fires says Mama

34= Selenium (Se) = **Sell** (Selenium) ed's knee after hit with hammer

35= Bromine (Br) = **Brooms** (Bromine) row a mile

36= Krypton (Kr) = **Krypton** (Krypton) rockets ignited by match

37= Rubidium (Rb)= **Rub** (Rubidium) back with a mug

38=Strontium (Sr)= **Strong**, (Strontium) red teabags move

39=Yttrium(Y)= **Yellow**, yes **yellow** T's (Yttrium) are on map

40=Zirconium (Zr)= **Zero** (Zirconium) riders own a horse

41=Niobium (Nb) = **Need** (Niobium) bees to rot

42=Molybdenum (Mo)= **Molly** (Molybdenum) opens den door to run

43=Technetium (Tc)= **Techno** (Technetium) color pictures fill the room

44=Ruthenium (Ru) = **Ruth** (Ruthenium) understands a lion's roar

45=Rhodium (Rh) = **Rhododendrons** (Rhodium) have blossoms, really

46=Palladium (Pd) = **Pals** (Palladium) decide who are rich

47=Silver (Ag) = **A g**audy **silver** (Silver) bracelet is in the rug

48=Cadmium (Cd) = **Caddie's** (Cadmium) dive for golf balls in the rough

49=Indium (In) = **Indians** (Indium) nabbed a rope

50=Tin (Sn) = **S**wimming **N**inja's stuck into **tin** (tin) wheels

51= Antimony (Sb) = **S**weet **b**uttery **ants** (Antimony) are thrown at the lady

52=Tellurium (Te) = **Tell** (Tellurium) everyone I'll be arriving alone

53=Iodine (I) **Iodine**, yes **Iodine**, covers a lamb

54= Xenon (Xe) = **X-Ray** escapes a lawyer

55=Caesium (Cs) = **Caesar** (Caesium) salads come from a lily

56=Barium (Ba) = **Bars** (Barium) are on a leash

57= Lanthanum (La) = **lanterns** (Lanthanum) attached to a log

58=Cerium (Ce) = **Cereals** (Cerium) eaten by lava

59=Praseodymium (Pr) = **Prayers** (Praseodymium) **r**educe cries of <u>help</u>

60=Neodymium (Nd) = **Needy** (Neodymium) **d**ogs eat <u>cheese</u>

61=Promethium (Pm) = **Promises** (Promethium) **m**ade keep mouths <u>shut</u>

62=Samarium (Sm) = **Sam** (Samarium) **m**akes a <u>chain</u>

63=Europium (Eu)= **Europe** (Europium) **u**nderstands <u>Jimmy</u>

64= Gadolinium (Gd) = **Glad** (Gadolinium) **d**ragons are full of good <u>cheer</u>

65=Terbium (Tb) = **Turban** (Terbium) **b**uried into a <u>shell</u>

66=Dysprosium (Dy) = **Dye** (Dysprosium) **y**ellow <u>choo choo</u>

67=Holmium (Ho) = **Holes** (Holmium) **o**pen and <u>shake</u>

68=Erbium (Er) = **Errors** (Erbium) **r**educe and <u>shave</u>

69=Thulium (Tm) = **Tools** (Thulium) **m**ade for a <u>ship</u>

70=Ytterbium (Yb)=**Yellow bees** (Ytterbium) begin to <u>kiss</u>

71=Lutetium (Lu) = **Let** (Lutetium) **U**ncle Tim fly the <u>kite</u>

72=Hafnium (Hf) = **Halfway** (Hafnium) **f**rom my <u>wagon</u>

73=Tantalum (Ta) = **Tan** (Tantalum) **a**corns make for a fun <u>game</u>

74=Tungsten (W)= **W**ag, yes **w**ag, **tongue** (Tungsten) around <u>car</u>

75=Rhenium (Re) = **Rinse** (Rhenium) **e**ggs from an <u>eagle</u>

76= Osmium (Os) = **Ozzie** (Osmium) **s**leeps on <u>couch</u>

77=Iridium (Ir) = **I rid** (Iridium) myself of a piece of <u>cake</u>

78=Platinium (Pt) = **Platforms** (Platinium) **t**ypically cause me to <u>cough</u>

79=Gold (Au)=**A**, **U**, here's some **gold** (Gold). It's yours to <u>keep</u>

80=Mercury (Hg)= **H**ave **g**asoline and drive a **Mercury** (Mercury) to <u>office</u>

81=Thalium (Tl) = **Tall Lee** (Thalium) ate <u>food</u>

82=Lead (Pb)= **P**olice **b**ought **lead** (Lead) pencils for <u>fun</u>

83=Bismuth (Bi) = **Busy** (Bismuth) **i**ndustries begin to <u>foam</u>

84=Polonium (Po) = **Poles** (Polonium) **o**nly catch on <u>fire</u>

85=Astatine (At) = **Ask Tina** (Astatine) to <u>fly</u>

86=Radon (Rn)= **Ray 'n Don** (Radon) <u>fish</u>

87=Francium (Fr) **France** (Francium) **r**eceives a <u>vac</u>

88=Radium (Ra) = **Razors** (Radium) **a**lways resemble a <u>fife</u>

89=Actinium (Ac) = **Actors** (Actinium) **c**an't be members of the <u>FBI</u>

90=Thorium (Th) = **Torn** (Thorium) **h**omes caused by the <u>bus</u>

91=Protactinium (Pa) = **Pro** (Protactinium) **a**thletes own the <u>boat</u>

92=Uranium (U)= **U**, yes **U**, **ran** (Uranium) to the <u>pony</u>

93=Neptunium (Np) = **Neptune** (Neptunium) **p**lays with a <u>bomb</u>

94=Plutonium (Pu) = **Pluto's** (Plutonium) **u**ncle is <u>poor</u>

95=Americium (Am)= **American** (Americium) **m**ade is red, white, and <u>blue</u>

96=Curium (Cm) = **Curious** (Curium) **m**onkeys hide in a <u>bush</u>

97= Berkelium (Bk) = **Brrr, Kevin** (Berkelium) is cold on his <u>bike</u>

98= Californium (Cf) = **California** (California) **f**ires don't <u>behave</u>

99=Einsteinium (Es)= **Einstein** (Einstein) **s**tudied like a <u>baby</u>

100=Fermium (Fm) = **Furs** (Fermium) **m**ake nice <u>daises</u>

101= Mendelevium (Md) = **Men delve** (Mendelevium) into every <u>test</u>

102=Nobelium (No) =**No,** (Nobelium) <u>o</u>nly bells stay at <u>Day's Inn</u>

103=Lawrencium (Lr) = **Laws** (Lawrencium) <u>r</u>egarding seas <u>daze me</u>

104=Rutherfordium (Rf) = **Ruts** (Rutherfordium) <u>f</u>illed by a <u>taser</u>

105=Dubnium (Db) = **Double** (Dubnium) <u>b</u>ony knees look like a <u>tassel</u>

106=Seaborgium (Sg) = **Seas** (Seaborgium) <u>g</u>o up, so grab <u>dosage</u>

107=Bohrium (Bh)= **Bows** (Bohrium) <u>h</u>it the <u>desk</u>

108=Hassium (Hs) = **Have some** (Hassium), don't <u>deceive</u>

109= Meitnerium (Mt)= **Meet** (Meitnerium) <u>t</u>hem at the <u>day spa</u>

110=Damstadium (Ds)= **Dams** (Damstadium) <u>s</u>tart by stadiums with <u>toads</u>

111=Roentgerium (Rg) = **Rents** (Roentgerium) <u>g</u>o up and are <u>dated</u>

112=Copernicium (Cn) = **Cops nick** (Copernicium) a <u>Titan</u>

113=Ununtrium (Uut) = **U, U, treat** (Ununtrium) nuns to lunch with <u>Tatum</u>

114= Flerovium (Fl) = **Fleas** (Flerovium) <u>l</u>eave by way of <u>detour</u>

115=Ununpertium (Uup) = **U, U, pretty** (Ununpertium) gal what's the <u>detail</u>

116=Livermorium (Lv)= **Liver** / (Livermorium) <u>v</u>egetables on a <u>hot dish</u>

117=Ununseptium (Uus) = **U, U** (Ununseptium) <u>s</u>upper is ready – <u>hot dog</u>

118=Ununoctium (Uuo) = **U, U, oh** (Ununoctium) knock off the <u>white dove</u>

To schedule the author for a consultation or as a speaker at your next function, contact …

Paul Mellor at paul@mellormemory.com

Or visit his website at …

www.mellormemory.com

Other books authored by Mr. Mellor include…

Finding the Keys for Remembering Anything
Memory Skills for Lawyers
How to Remember Bible Verses
You Have the Right to Remember (police)
You're Almost There
Road to the White House
Pathway to the Podium

Made in the USA
Middletown, DE
20 November 2019

79121156R00080